THE
GOD
WE
SEEK

Portraits *of* God
in the Old Testament

MARY DONOVAN TURNER

CHALICE®
PRESS

ST. LOUIS, MISSOURI

Cover art: iStockphoto
Cover and interior design: Elizabeth Wright

Visit Chalice Press on the World Wide Web at
www.chalicepress.com

10 9 8 7 6 5 4 3 2 1   11   12   13   14   15

EPUB: 978-08272-12725   EPDF: 978-08272-12732

Library of Congress Cataloging–in–Publication Data

Turner, Mary Donovan.
   The God we seek : portraits of God in the Old Testament / Mary Donovan Turner. — 1st ed.
      p. cm.
   Includes bibliographical references and index.
   ISBN 978-0-8272-1251-0 (pbk.)
   1. God--Biblical teaching. 2. Bible. O.T.—Criticism, interpretation, etc. I. Title. II. Title: Portraits of God in the Old Testament.

BS1192.6.T87 2010
231'.044—dc22   2010034917

Printed in the United States of America

Contents

Introduction   1
The Wondrous World of Metaphor   6

    Anointing One   9
    Buckler   11
    Cloud   13
    Comforter   15
    Compassionate One   17
    Creator   20
    Dawn   22
    Deliverer   23
    Dew   25
    Eagle   27
    Enemy   29
    Father   31
    Father of Orphans   34
    Fire   36
    Fortress   38
    Friend   39
    God Almighty/*El Shaddai*   40
    Healer   42
    Helper   44
    Hiding Place   45
    Holy One   46
    Hunter   48
    Husband   49
    Judge   51
    Leopard, Lion, Mother Bear   52
    Light   54
    Maggots/Moth/Rottenness   55

Midwife Ps 22.9-10; Is. 46,3-4 56
Mother/Woman Giving Birth   58
My Chosen Portion/My Cup   59
Parent   60
Potter   62
Prosecutor   63
Protector of Widows   64
Redeemer   66
Refuge   67
Rock   68
Salvation   70
Shade/Shadow   72
Shepherd   73
Shower   75
Song   76
Stronghold of the Oppressed   78
Suffering One   79
Sun   80
Sustainer   81
The One Who Lifts Up My Head   82
Vineyard Owner   83
Voice   83
Warrior   85
Wrestler   86

Afterthoughts   89
Questions for Reflection   91
Metaphors and Ministry—Dr. Archie Smith Jr.   119
Notes   135
Index of Biblical Citations   139

Introduction

A drop of dew on the early morning landscape? The sound of sheer silence? A piercing light that shatters night darkness? A loud thunderous voice whose power can bend a sturdy tree to the ground? A boulder? Firm foundation? A wide and spacious place on which to stand? Who is God? What is God? What kinds of words can be used to describe our experiences with God? Perhaps you can make a list of the many words and phrases that you or your church communities use to describe "who God is." It may be that you have had congregational conversations about the "pictures"[1] or metaphors used for God in worship and study. Which are appropriate? Which are inappropriate? When? Where? Why are we so different in our understandings? Though there may be disagreement about which metaphors are right or appropriate, metaphors are indispensable to our theological work.[2]

A journey through the Old Testament teaches us that no one name or metaphor for God can say all that there is to say about God, about mystery or the unknown.[3] In different social and political eras, historical periods and in local contexts, people of faith used varying words to try to describe the God with whom they were in relationship. Some of these names for God became common, and we find them appearing and reappearing in different kinds of biblical literature over time. Other metaphors appear only once in the Hebrew Scriptures; the writer seemingly, in the moment, had to find a new way to describe and define what God was doing in the world. Together, the list of metaphors in this volume provides a delightful panorama of understandings, though not an exhaustive one. The list is challenging and complicated; one understanding opposes and seems to negate others. There is tension and paradox.[4] And yet there are great learnings here for us:

1. One human word cannot say all that is to be said about God. Our language is too limited and finite. Thus, often the psalmists used a long list of metaphors and names for God. One just would

not do. "I love you, O LORD, my strength. / The LORD is my rock, my fortress, and my deliverer, / my God, my rock in whom I take refuge, / my shield, and the horn of my salvation, my stronghold. / I call upon the LORD, who is worthy to be praised, / so I shall be saved from my enemies" (Ps. 18:1–3). Count them. There are, in the first three verses of this psalm, at least *seven* different metaphors used for God, each emphasizing a different characteristic or aspect of experience. What is the experience of reading these together?

2.   Local contexts and different life experiences give rise to different, favorite names for God. Second Isaiah, for instance, who needed to convince the exilic community that God could and would save them, repeatedly used the metaphors of "creator" and "redeemer." A creator has great power. Second Isaiah's message, then, was that the God who created them was powerful enough to save them. A redeemer has a desire to deliver people from their despair. The God who created them was powerful enough and desired to save them. That was God's intention.

3.   Worship is enriched when we realize that we have at our disposal many biblical metaphors for God. Using them allows those in the community to become acquainted with them. It also invites community members to find those that are most meaningful at their own place and time. Who decides what metaphors to use in your own worshiping community? Are they inclusive? Are they diverse?

Ultimately, the metaphors we explore here are important because it is imperative not only that we believe in God, but that we understand the kind of God we believe in! This discernment matters. What the church can be and do in the world depends on a clear naming of *who* God is. Israel did not offer to us a finished or polished portrayal of God. There are testimonies, and there are testimonies that disagree with other testimonies. There is an unsettled portrait painted for us: unsettled and unsettling. This is an ambiguous picture of God we have received from our ancestors of faith.[5] On the one hand we have a lively God. This God is mobile. This God acts and reacts, utters threats and withdraws them, turning from wrath to grace. On the other, we witness in the Old Testament a strong tradition that attests to God's unchangeableness. The roots of this tradition spread far and wide.[6]

The danger, of course, is that a person or a community can decide to be content with only a few metaphors for God. When that happens, the community can ultimately decide that these are the "right ones." This understanding stifles conversation and the imagination. It isolates us from the wealth our biblical tradition affords us. And, ultimately, it may alienate or isolate those whose understandings and experiences need or must find different expression.

Understanding the contextual and local nature of metaphors brings to the forefront a question that can polarize worshiping communities. Is there a time when metaphors that have served a community of people in a particular place and time need to be "retired"? Can the metaphors that have been inherited from our tradition cause damage or oppression? When do we let them go and embrace new, inclusive, life-giving ones? How do we decide?

Because the biblical text is open to such a great diversity in language, it invites us to find our own. Biblical or not, our words make it possible, even if only partially, to name our experiences. Named experiences can be shared. Named experiences can create community as similarities and differences are explored. Through conversation, truth is discovered. *The God we seek* is, then, an invitation not only to explore the world of the ancient Israelites but also to think critically about one's own experiences of God. It is an invitation to re-imagine, to explore and reflect on the God whose we are.

It is important, first, to consider the many names for God in the Old Testament. We need to know about them and understand the differences that they hold so that we can be attentive to them:

Yahweh (YHWH)—This name occurs almost seven thousand times in the Old Testament. It is translated LORD in most English Bibles. What does this word mean and where did it come from? Different sources tell us varied things, but it most likely comes from a form of the Hebrew verb "to be." It can be translated in a variety of ways. In Exodus 3:14, Moses asks God to tell him his name. God responds with *"Yahweh."* This can mean, "I am who I am," or, "I will be who

I will be," or even, "He causes to be what exists." The name remains "tantalizingly unreadable."[7] The scribes of the ancient Hebrew texts preserved only the consonants of this name, Yahweh, for us. This was to discourage people from saying the name; the name of God was far too sacred. This God is a patriarchal one, and, as we will find out when we explore other metaphors in this volume, a violent one.

Elohim—This word occurs about twenty-five hundred times in the Old Testament. The word is plural, and sometimes it is translated "gods." Most often, however, it is considered a name of greatness and power and majesty for the one God of Israel and is translated simply as "God."

El—El is used about two hundred times and is also translated God. This is the common name for God in ancient near eastern cultures. Every divine being had this name. It is generic, so to speak, and, while it was used in other cultures, the Israelites adopted it as their own.

There are other names for God in the Old Testament. *El Elyon* (God Most High), *El Olam* (God of Eternity), *El Berith* (God of the Covenant) and *El Roi* (God of seeing).[8]

This is a great adventure. We are seeking to know about a God with many names. We want to understand the God that was known by people who lived hundreds and thousands of years ago. Yet, we stand on the shoulders of our ancestors of faith. In ways we understand and in ways we do not, they are our foundation. What metaphors did this people use to try to name their own experiences of God? And what can we learn from them?

One of your biggest surprises may be the number of metaphors that bring us pictures of a grace-filled, faithful and loving God. Many in the Christian community hold stereotyped understandings of the God of the Old Testament; they understand this God to be filled only with wrath and judgment—a vindictive, punitive God.[9] They will be surprised at the ways the text bears witness to a loving God who longs to be in relationship with the covenant people. These contrasting images of God may be difficult to reconcile.

The following pages will contain some common metaphors, or "pictures," for God. Some will surprise and even startle you. There are nearly sixty in all. What do they whisper to us across the centuries? What can we learn? How will we be inspired?

At the conclusion of this volume is an article written by Dr. Archie Smith Jr., the James and Clarice Foster Professor of Pastoral Psychology and Counseling at the Pacific School of Religion and Graduate Theological Union in Berkeley, California. Professor Smith defines and demonstrates for us the value of metaphors, ancient and contemporary, in the practice of ministry. "The Skyline Has Changed; A Big Tree has Fallen" invites us to think about the importance of words and language in our communities of faith.

The Wondrous World
of Metaphor

"God is my rock…" Think about this very simple statement. We find it in the Psalms along with other statements like it. The psalmists and the prophets and those telling the stories of ancient Israel try to find ways to talk about God that will help those who hear and read their words to know something of the speaker/writer's experience of God. "God is my rock." The biblical writer knows that God is not a rock, but in the writer's mind there is something about God that is like a rock. He says God is like rock because he does not know any other way to talk about God; he must use words and phrases that arise out of the experience of living to communicate who God is.

That is how a metaphor works. It describes "this" in terms of "that" so that we can understand "this" more clearly. There is a thread of similarity between God and rock. The association between the two is open. There is not one right answer to the question: Why is God like a rock? or *How* is God like a rock? The psalmists themselves seem to have different answers to that question. One implies that God is like a rock because rocks are strong and unchanging. Another says God is like a rock because a rock lends a much firmer foundation than shifting sand. When God is like a rock, we have a stable foundation on which we can stand.

Interestingly, these are not the only explanations given by the psalmists for why God is like a rock. For several, God is like a rock, not because rocks are firm and unchanging, but because rocks have crevices, clefts. The psalmists envisioned the rock's cleft as a place to hide from the enemy and all the tribulations that life was bringing to them.

Saying that God is a like a rock does not say everything that needs to be said about God. "Rock" highlights some important aspects of the nature of God, but it minimizes others. It does not, for instance, imply relationship nor does it paint a picture of grace or righteousness or justice. Still, it communicates an important message to us.

"God is my rock." What, then, does that statement mean to you? Is it your experience of God? Thinking about the metaphor can open our imaginations to other people's experiences of God, and our own. Working with metaphors, we can converse about God; it opens new opportunities for us to tell our stories. Theologizing is a communal affair! We converse, allowing all voices into the conversation in order to discern truths for our living.

Our metaphors matter. It is no longer helpful simply to ask the question: Do you believe in God? It is important also to ask: *What kind* of God do you believe in? Our answers to that question are filled with metaphors and our attempts to describe to ourselves and the community the God that we know. The metaphor stands between mystery and meaning. Metaphors are vital. They open new arenas of understanding. They can be shocking and revolutionary.

The Hebrew Bible uses many metaphors for God. Some of them you will find in this volume. Look at the long list in the Table of Contents. How are the metaphors like each other and how are they different? Are there tensions between them? How many of the metaphors are "human" metaphors that imply something about relationship and family? How many of them are inanimate objects that we encounter in our lives? Which ones are familiar and which are not? Which describe your own experience and language? What did the metaphors mean in the ancient world? When an Israelite praying in the temple talked about God as "rock," did she mean the same thing as we mean when we talk about God in the same way?

Our religious language is metaphorical because we do not have other ways to talk about who God is. We have no words and no phrases that can describe the fullness of God. And so we try, with the words we have, to name the God whose we are. On the following pages there are metaphors for God. There are also metaphors that try to describe God's work in the world. There are other words and phrases, not metaphors in the strictest sense of the word, but "pictures" of the God our ancestors knew and worshiped.

And so we read what they have written and find ourselves on the wondrous journey of finding our own language, individually and in community, for the God we seek.

Anointing One

Samuel took a vial of oil and poured it on his head, and kissed him; he said, "The LORD has anointed you ruler over his people Israel. You shall reign over the people of the LORD and you will save them from the hand of their enemies all around.
1 Samuel 10:1

The spirit of the Lord GOD is upon me, / because the LORD has anointed me; / he has sent me to bring good news to the oppressed, / to bind up the brokenhearted, / to proclaim liberty to the captives, / and release to the prisoners; / to proclaim the year of the LORD's favor, / and the day of vengeance of our God, / to comfort all who mourn; / to provide for those who mourn in Zion— / to give them a garland instead of ashes, / the oil of gladness instead of mourning, / the mantle of praise instead of a faint spirit. Isaiah 61:1—3

The Israelites' land was dry. Skin could become very "leathery" in the searing heat. Oil would often be applied to soften the skin or protect it from the arid environment. This important practice was soothing and comforting and refreshing to those who received it. The oil could protect wounds; it could aid in healing. This was an informal practice of anointing one's family member, a friend, or a weary stranger passing through.[1]

The formal practice of anointing by pouring oil on the head was used to commission, designate, and set apart a person for a certain function or role in the community. People or things could be consecrated and dedicated to God for their special purposes. A simple read through Exodus, where it describes how the Tent of Meeting was being constructed and furnished, illustrates how every part of the worship space was anointed for its own unique purpose. It was consecrated for the part it would play in the worship drama. In chapter 40 we are told that Yahweh spoke to Moses and told him in great detail how to erect the tabernacle and carefully place the furnishings inside. The ark of the covenant went into the tent, and was to be screened by a curtain. Moses was to bring in the table, the settings, lamp stand, golden altar, and the basin with water. Then Moses was to anoint the tabernacle and all that was in it, all of its furniture, so that it would become holy. To be holy was to be set aside and consecrated for divine purpose. Then Aaron and his sons were to come, put on their sacred, priestly vestments, and they also were to be anointed and consecrated so that they could serve. In this same way prophets and kings were anointed.

Later in 1 Samuel Yahweh spoke to Samuel and told him to fill his horn with oil and to set out. Samuel was sent to Jesse in Bethlehem because, God said, "I have provided for myself a king among his sons" (1 Sam. 16:1). Samuel objected, being fearful of the king Saul, who might hear that a new king was being anointed to dethrone him. He was afraid for his life. But Samuel went and found Jesse and his sons and invited them to a sacrifice. As the sons presented themselves, Samuel tried to guess which one might be the chosen one of God. Perhaps, he thought, Eliab. Surely this is the one chosen to be king; Eliab was tall and strong. But God said to Samuel, "Do not look on his appearance or on the height of his stature, because I have rejected him; for the Lord does not see as mortals see; they look on the outward appearance, but the Lord looks on the heart" (v. 7). Jesse made seven of his sons pass by in front of Samuel, but Samuel said that the Lord had chosen none of these. "Are all your sons here?" (v. 11a), Samuel asked. And Jesse said, "There remains yet the youngest, but he is keeping the sheep" (v. 11b). So Jesse sent for David and he came. He was ruddy and handsome, and "The Lord said, 'Rise and anoint him'" (v. 12).

David, of course, was not the most likely choice. He was the youngest, not the oldest, son. He was not the tallest; nor was he the strongest. He was the unlikely choice, but he was God's choice. And Samuel took the horn of oil, and anointed him in the presence of his brothers. It is written that "the spirit of the Lord came mightily upon David from that day forward" (v. 13). At the time of anointing, God empowers persons with a spirit that enables them to do the job for which they have been called.

The anointed one was authorized and empowered to do God's work in the world, even when, in the world's eyes, that person was the least likely. Are we all anointed, called and empowered to do God's work? Can God's spirit be released within and through us? As preachers, teachers, social workers, builders, musicians, artists, parents...?

In the book of Isaiah, the prophet says that God's spirit is upon him and that the Lord has anointed him to bring good news to the oppressed, bind up the brokenhearted, proclaim liberty to the captives and release to the prisoners, proclaim the year of the Lord's favor and vengeance, comfort all who mourn, and provide for those who mourn in Zion (Isaiah 61:1–2). The prophet is anointed and thus empowered for this task. In Luke, the gospel writer uses these words to inaugurate the ministry of Jesus (Lk. 4:18–19). Jesus speaks these words in the synagogue and says that they are, that day, fulfilled. Jesus is the Messiah (the anointed one) and the purposes of his ministry and mission are set forth for the gospel readers. As the gospel story unfolds we witness the anointed one bringing good news, liberty, and comfort to those he meets along the way. We are a called people. How are you and your community called and anointed for the ministries that Jesus himself embraced?

Buckler

*But you, O Lord, are a shield [buckler] around me...*Psalm 3:3

Our soul waits for the Lord; / he is our help and shield.
Psalm 33:20

For the Lord gives wisdom; / from his mouth come knowledge and understanding; / he stores up sound wisdom for the upright; / he is a shield to those who walk blamelessly. Proverb 2:6–7

The word is certainly not a part of most people's every day vocabulary: *buckler*. What does it mean? *Buckler* is a military term. It describes a large shield that soldiers took with them for protection in the time of battle. For those who walk blamelessly or for those who are willing to take refuge there, God is the shield in time of trouble.

A shield is important for those who feel that they are battling the world; who feel that the forces are against them; who know those around them ridicule them; or who face overwhelming tasks. That is why, no doubt, these words come to Abram from Yahweh as they are making a covenant with one another: "Do not be afraid, Abram, I am your shield; your reward shall be very great" (Gen. 15:1).

In Psalm 115, the psalmist speaks convincingly of the power and greatness of the Israelite God in contrast to the idols that are worshiped by the Israelites' neighbors. The idols are made by human hands of silver and gold. The idols have mouths but do not speak; they have eyes but do not see; ears, but they do not hear; noses, but they do not smell; hands, but they do not feel; feet, but they do not walk. And they have throats but they do not speak; they have no voice. The difference, then, between the idols and the God worshiped by the Israelites is that their God does see, hear, feel, smell, and speak. This God can move from place to place. In sum, their God is a living, moving, breathing presence in their lives. This God is dynamic, still creating. This God has agency and can effect change. This God can save them, help them, and deliver them from harm.

The psalmist then pleads to Israel, to the house of Aaron, and then to all who trust in Yahweh. Here is a dependable source of trust. In this God they can be confident. Three times the psalmist repeats, "He is their help and their shield" (vv. 9, 10, 11). The repetition of this line alerts us to what is really important for the psalmist and the worshipers he addresses. The Lord is their shield, their buckler. This God *will* protect because, unlike the idols, this God *can* protect. The metaphor of the shield expresses for the psalmist a trust in the capability and desire of God to be with the people.

Those who cry out in the Psalms know that God, their shield, is the place where they can find refuge and salvation.

There is an interesting twist on this "picture" of God in Psalm 35. The psalmist doesn't cry out to a God who is like a shield; the psalmist cries out to God to take up a shield: "Contend, O Lord, with those who contend with me; fight against those who fight against me! Take hold of shield and buckler, and rise up to help me!" (v. 2). The psalmist is simply saying to God, "Fight for me!" Fight with me.

The buckler is the God of those who are in foxholes or on the battle lines, the God of those who know many enemies or constant oppression. It is the God of those who face whatever threatens to destroy them.

Thus the "buckler" is an interesting metaphor for God. It comes from the world of war; it is a military term. The shield is what the Israelites and those around them have taken into battle. And yet, as the image is used in the Psalms, it speaks something of quiet refuge. The shield provides security and safety. It is a place where we can rest.

This image of God raises interesting and thorny theological issues. Does God protect us, shield us, from injury and harm? What does your own life experience tell you? Or does God walk with us when harm comes our way? Exploring our own answers to these questions gives us important clues to our understandings of how God is at work in our world.

Cloud

I will quietly look from my dwelling / like clear heat in sunshine, / like a cloud of dew in the heat of harvest. Isaiah 18:4

It had only been a very short time since the Israelites crossed through the Red Sea and found themselves safely settled on the other side of the large, foreboding body of water. Moses sang. Miriam and all the women danced. God had brought them safely out of the hands of their oppressors and was leading them to a new place: home.

Only three days into the wilderness of Shur they found themselves with no drinkable water. "What shall we drink?" they asked. Water was made sweet, and the people were then led to Elim where there were twelve springs of water and palm trees. They camped there.

The people were then led to the wilderness of Sin between Elim and Sinai; this was on the fifteenth day of the second month after they had departed from Egypt. They were hungry; there was now no food. "Why did you bring us out into the wilderness to die?" they asked their leader Moses (see Ex. 16:3). Again God promised to be with them—to bring quail for them by night and bread for them each morning, for God had heard their complaining.

Moses said to his brother Aaron, "Say to the whole congregation of the Israelites, 'Draw near to the LORD, for he has heard your complaining'" (v. 9). And as Aaron spoke to the whole congregation, and as they looked out into the wilderness, they saw the glory of the LORD in a cloud.

Picturing God as a cloud is enormously rich and instructive to us. Nearly fifty times in the story of the wilderness wandering we find either God or God's glory appearing in the form of a cloud. What could be a more helpful image of God than this? The people are traveling through the wilderness; their journey is long and grueling. The sand stings and briars scratch, and as they walk a cloud appears as an image of hope. Clouds mean water for their dry, thirsty throats. Clouds potentially bring shade from the blazing sun.

As the Jewish rabbis thought about the cloud that God used to guide their ancestors—the Israelites—through the wilderness, they imagined what the wondrous nature of the guiding cloud was. In thinking about Exodus 13:21, one rabbi asked, "How many clouds of glory encompassed Israel in the wilderness?" The answer was seven clouds. One on each side of the Israelites while they traveled, one beneath them, one above them, and one going out before them raising every lowland and lowering every highland to make the pathway level to walk on. As the cloud advanced, it was thought that perhaps also the cloud killed snakes and scorpions, sweeping them away, while also sprinkling the road to calm the dust that swirled around them. For the rabbis, the cloud was a protective and helpful presence.[2]

God wants to convince the people that though the journey is difficult God will be there.

As the people travel, it is a cloud that leads them. It is a cloud that signals God's presence with them. It is a cloud that covers the top of the mountain as Moses goes up to receive the commandments. It is a cloud that settles down over the tabernacle, a signal that God is moving with them as they take step after step to a land they hope is out there before them, but which they have never seen. The cloud signals the promise that something good awaits them.

The cloud imagery finds its way into prophetic literature. Particularly interesting is Isaiah 25, where the prophet describes the great banquet to be held at the end time, the time of redemption for the poor and the needy. This banquet will be a feast of rich foods and good wines. Death will be swallowed and tears will be wiped away from all faces.

This poem in Isaiah celebrates and anticipates the day when the weak will be saved from their mighty oppressors. The cities of the powerful oppressors will be destroyed, left in ruins, and they will know that those who oppress will not, in the end, prevail. God is a refuge of the poor and needy in their distress. To these, God is a shelter from the rainstorm, the assaults from the ruthless. God is like the shade from the clouds drawing over those who have been used and abused.

Interestingly, the prophet Hosea also uses the metaphor of the cloud to describe the love the people have for their God, but this is a fickle, not steadfast, love! (6:4). The people love God like a morning cloud, a cloud that dissipates and dissolves when the morning light comes upon it. It is here, and then it is not. The people's love for God comes and then it quickly goes. It is not like the love that God has for us—faithful and forever sure.

Comforter

But you, O Lord, are a God merciful and gracious, / slow to anger and abounding in steadfast love and faithfulness. / Turn to me and be gracious to me; / give your strength to your servant; / save the child of your serving girl. / Show me a sign of your favor, / so that those who hate me may see it and be put to shame, / because you, Lord, have helped me and comforted me.
Psalm 86:15–17

It is the initial rousing cry of Second Isaiah: "Comfort, O comfort my people, says your God. / Speak tenderly to Jerusalem, and cry to her / that she has served her term, / that her penalty is paid, / that she has received from the Lord's hand / double for all her sins" (Isa. 40:1). It is, at first, a wonderful image of the caring, compassionate, comforting God. God sees the distress of Jerusalem, which has been destroyed. God hears the cries of those who are now in exile, torn away from their homeland and from the temple. They are now living in a land foreign and unfamiliar, and God has heard them.

This is a picture of comfort, but it is also a blatant picture of despair and of those who are in need of comfort. They live with challenging and difficult questions. Has their plight and their misery come to them through the hand of God? Is God the one who brings the despair *and* also the comfort from it?

The word *comfort* implies such thinking. There is something wrong that is made right. Despair turns into hope. Pain turns into healing. God, who has brought their destruction, now brings their comfort. In some of its forms the word translated "comfort" is translated "repent." God repents. God changes God's mind. In the Genesis flood story, God "repents" that God has made the people (Gen. 6:6). Later God repents that God has made Saul king (1 Sam. 15:11).

In Jeremiah we read that the people are in great despair. God cries out again and again that God will not "repent of the evil" that has been done to them. ("Because of this, the earth shall mourn, / and the heavens above grow black; / for I have spoken, I have purposed; / I have not relented nor will I turn back" [Jer. 4:28].) God is angry at the people's unfaithfulness. God's intention is to destroy. God is unrelenting. God will not comfort.

But then, of course, God does change: "Thus says the LORD, the God of Israel, to whom you sent me to present your plea before him: If you will only remain in this land, then I will build you up and not pull you down; I will plant you, and not pluck you up, for I am sorry [I repent] for the disaster that I have brought upon you" (Jer. 42:9–10). God is emotionally involved.

Comfort implies a change, then, from something wrong, bad, or frightening to something different and better. In Psalm 23 the worshiper is walking through a dark valley, and it is God's rod and staff that bring comfort. In Ruth, Boaz brings comfort to Ruth by speaking kindly to her and by delivering her from a life of insecurity and want.

God provides comfort in different ways. Sometimes comfort comes through a supportive word from a friend or family member.

Sometimes it may come through a sermon, sometimes through moments of rest and relief from stress and constant challenge. For the psalmist in Psalm 77 it comes through remembering.

The psalmist is suffering; the psalmist cries out, and seeks and stretches out his hand to God so that he can be delivered from his despair. But in the end, he says, "my soul refuses to be comforted" (v. 2). The psalmist thinks of God, moans, and faints. He cannot sleep; he cannot speak. And, in the darkness, questions come to haunt him. Has he been cast off from Yahweh? Has God forgotten to extend God's grace? Has God's compassion been cut off by God's anger?

The psalmist meditates and thinks and reflects about God. Where is God? It is in remembering that the psalmist finds his comfort. The psalmist begins to remember the stories of old, how God performed mighty acts to deliver the psalmist's ancestors from their oppressions and despair. He remembers how God brought the Israelites through the waters, though they were very afraid. And though God's footprints were unseen (v. 19), it surely was God who saved and redeemed them. God led God's people and brought them comfort. Knowing that God has delivered the ancestors of old brought comfort to the psalmist in his current suffering and pain.

When the Israelites were taken from their homes and carried away to Babylon, they were in exile and in great despair. The prophet known as Second Isaiah brought a word of comfort to them. (See Isa. 49:13; 51:3; 52:9.) To those who knew one of life's greatest tragedies came these words: "As a mother comforts her child, / so I will comfort you; / you shall be comforted in Jerusalem" (Isa. 66:13).

One of the most beautiful pictures in the world is the mother comforting a child who has had a bad dream, who skins a knee, who is lonely and estranged from friends, who is feeling "left out."

God comforts God's people. Perhaps comfort, not tragedy, is the final word.

Compassionate One

*Gracious is the L*ORD*, and righteous; / our God is [compassionate]. / The L*ORD *protects the simple; / when I was brought low, he saved me. / Return, O my soul, to your rest, for* *the LORD has dealt bountifully with you. / For you have delivered my soul from death, / my eyes from tears, / my feet from stumbling.* Psalm 116:5–8

Tender mercies—a soft and gentle phrase that is used to describe what God grants to those why cry out for compassion. "Do not, O LORD, withhold your mercy from me; / let your steadfast love and your faithfulness / keep me safe forever" (Ps. 40:11). Sometimes translated "mercy," or "tender mercy," or "pity," or "compassion," this word in Hebrew is related to the word for womb. The womb protects and nourishes, but it does not possess and control. It yields so that the well-being and wholeness may happen. It provides a secure and safe environment.

Many stories in the Old Testament show us how human beings show compassion for one another. Joseph feels compassion burning inside himself when he first meets his brother Benjamin, son of his mother (Gen. 43:30; 45:14). It is the essence of the story in 1 Kings 3:16–28 about King Solomon. Two prostitutes come and stand before him. One of them says to him:

> "This woman and I live in the same house; and I gave birth while she was in the house. Then on the third day after I gave birth, this woman also gave birth. We were together; there was no one else with us in the house, only the two of us... Then this woman's son died in the night, because she lay on him. She got up in the middle of the night and took my son from beside me while your servant slept. She laid him at her breast and laid her dead son at my breast. When I rose in the morning to nurse my son, I saw that he was dead; but when I looked at him closely in the morning, clearly it was not the son I had borne." (vv. 17–21)

An argument follows. Each of the two women claims the living son as her own.

The dilemma is clearly set before the king; the difficulty of making a sound and fair judgment is evident. The king orders a sword and says, "Divide the living boy in two; then give half to the one, and half to the other" (v. 25). The true mother cries out, wanting to save the life of her child. She says "Give her the living boy; certainly do not kill him!" But the other said, "It shall be neither mine or yours; divide it" (v. 26). The mother identified herself by her compassion. She demonstrates her womblike love. Because her compassion grew warm, the mother was willing to forfeit justice for the sake of her child's life. Finally, the woman is called mother; her love has been exposed. Ultimately, we come to understand that the love of the prostitute for her child and the love Joseph has for his brother is the same kind of compassion that God has for us. Isaiah 49:15 uses this word to speak of a mother's love toward her nursing child and, consequently, God's love for us. The Psalms use it to describe the love of a father, and, ultimately, God's love for us. "As a father has compassion for his children, / so [Yahweh] has compassion for those who fear [Yahweh]" (Ps. 103:13).

Hosea uses the metaphors of God as husband *and* God ultimately as parent to paint the picture of God as the compassionate one, though the first images in the story are difficult and offensive. Too often they are used to justify abuse! In the first two chapters of Hosea, the prophet tells a story about Hosea and Gomer. Yahweh tells Hosea to marry a "wife of whoredom." As the story of the relationship between Hosea is told, the reader becomes aware that Hosea symbolizes God; Gomer the community of God's people. Hosea marries Gomer, and they have three children: two sons and a daughter. The daughter is named "No Compassion." Gomer, an adulteress, comes to symbolize the faithless, wandering people of Israel who break their covenant relationship with God. The daughter "No Compassion" symbolizes the relationship God has with the unfaithful people. God will have "no compassion" for them.

In chapter 2, God recounts God's anger and what will happen to the people who have been unfaithful. Verses 6, 9, and 14 all begin with the word translated as "therefore." Each recounts a response God will have toward the unfaithful wife, the people. In verses 6ff, God will build a wall around her so that she cannot find her lovers. In verses 9ff, God will uncover her shame and strip her naked. God will punish her. The reader expects another indictment and punishment in verse 14, but what we witness there is neither of these. The reader finds a startling word of compassion and grace. "Therefore, I will now allure her, / and bring her into the wilderness, / and speak tenderly to her." God moves forward to reestablish a relationship with the people; this is a word of forgiveness and restoration. In the end, God is compassionate, but we are left to wonder—does the final word of reconciliation mediate the appalling and graphic descriptions of the abusive and violent behaviors perpetrated against the wife?

In Hosea 11, God shows compassion for Israel just as a parent shows compassion and forgiveness for a child. God has nurtured the community, carried them, and fed them like children. They turn away, but God's heart recoils, and then God reacts with compassion that is warm and tender. God cannot give them up. God will not execute God's anger. God is the compassionate one who answers the cries of those in need and surrounds them with concern. Just as the mother and father hear their child who cries out in the darkness, God hears us when we are lost or afraid.

Creator

Have you not known? Have you not heard? / The LORD is the everlasting God, / the Creator of the ends of the earth. He does not faint or grow weary; / his understanding is unsearchable. / He gives power to the faint, / and strengthens the powerless. / Even youths will faint and be weary, / and the young will fall exhausted; / but those who wait for the LORD shall renew their strength, / they shall mount up with wings like eagles, / they shall run and not be weary, / they shall walk and not faint.
Isaiah 40:28–31

Sometimes it happens when we look up into the heavens and see a host of small lights emanating from stars that we know are millions of miles away. Sometimes it happens when we stand on the sandy seashore and look out at the crashing waves and waters that seemingly have no end. Or sometimes it happens when we look at the intricacies of a spiraling DNA, the blueprint for our lives, and realize how complicated and interrelated are all of our parts. It is then that we ask: Is there something or someone who has created all of this? Someone or something that hurled galaxies out into space and formed and fashioned the newly born son or daughter resting comfortably in the hospital nursery? Is God the creator of all that is and will be?

This same sense of awe and wonder about the world bursts forth from the psalmist in Psalm 8: "When I look at your heavens, the work of your fingers, / the moon and the stars that you have established..." (v. 3). The bigness and greatness of the world makes the psalmist feel insignificant and small.

If it is God who created us, God would know us. To that end, one psalmist thinks about the God who has formed his inward parts and who has knit him together in his mother's womb (Ps. 139). This is the God who has searched and known him. This is the God who can discern his thoughts even from far away. This is the God who is acquainted with all his ways. The God who creates is one who is intimately involved with the lives that have been created. This is a God who is everywhere; there is no place one can flee from God's Spirit.

The God who can create and renew the world is also a God who is powerful. In the midst of exile and great despair, when the Israelites had lost their land, their temple, and their home place, a prophet rose up among them. This was a prophet who was bringing a fresh word of good news and hope to them. This God who has created every living thing, Second Isaiah said to the exiles, is strong and mighty. The one who has created every end of the earth does not grow faint or weary. The one who created us lends us power and strength when we are exhausted and grow weary (Isa. 40:25–31). In the end, the one who is powerful enough to have created us is powerful enough to deliver us out of oppression.

Is God still creating? Just as surely as the Old Testament attests to a God that has created the world, it testifies to a God that is creating still though we are not aware or alert to the newness that springs forth. What is God creating in your life? In the life of the community?

The Old Testament begins with two stories of creation. The first, in Genesis 1, starts: "In the beginning when God created the heavens and the earth..." In this story, God created the world in six days. God rests on the seventh day and, according to the storyteller, ushers in the ritual of Sabbath keeping. God is portrayed as a powerful God, who can create the whole cosmos—the earth and the heavens—simply by speaking. All that God has created is pronounced as "good." Finally, on the sixth day, humankind is created in God's image. God looks upon all that is created; together all that is created is deemed "very good."

The second story of creation takes place in the garden of Eden. In this story, humans are created first. God in this story is more immediate and personal, planting and walking through the garden, talking with Adam and Eve.

These two creation stories together portray both the powerful creating God and the close, intimate, creating God—the God who knows us and the God who is powerful enough to redeem and deliver us. Both these understandings of the creator God are woven throughout the remainder of the Old Testament.

Dawn

Let us know, let us press on to know the Lord*; / his appearing is as sure as the dawn; / he will come to us like the showers, / like the spring rains that water the earth.* Hosea 6:3

The dawn, when the first pinkish threads of light come streaking across the sky, can be glorious. It signals the end of the night and the beginning of the new day that can bring opportunity and a renewed chance for hopefulness. Dawn is a time of transition. It is a time between the passing night and coming day. It is a time and space for hope, anticipation, and the opening of new beginnings and possibilities. But it is not the beauty or new beginnings that the dawn signals for the prophet Hosea. It is certainty. It is steadfastness.

In the beginning of the book of Ecclesiastes, the writer is recounting the consistent, never-changing aspects of the world around us. He says there is nothing new under the sun. A generation comes, he says, and then it dies. Another comes and goes. This process goes on forever. He talks about the wind that blows from the north; then the south. Then it blows from the north again. It always returns. Streams and rivers run to the sea. The sea never fills but the streams and river are always, always flowing. The sun rises and the sun goes down. Then the sun hurries around the earth only to rise once more. There is always the dawn and always the sunset. It is this kind of consistency that the prophet Hosea has in mind when talks about God appearing to us. God is, Hosea says, as sure as the dawn. We can count on God coming to be with us. Always.

The prophet is calling the people to return to their God. He knows that, though they are broken, God remains the source of their strength. God will bind up the people, revive and resurrect them so that they can again have life. "Let us know, let us press on to know the LORD: / his appearing is as sure as the dawn..." (Hos. 6:3). Just as surely as the sun makes its way over the horizon every morning, so God will be ready to meet the people who have turned away but are ready to return home.

Deliverer

Yet you are holy, / enthroned on the praises of Israel. / In you our ancestors trusted; / they trusted, and you delivered them. / To you they cried, and were saved; / in you they trusted, and were not put to shame. Psalm 22:3–5

The psalmist suffers. It is a personal suffering; he speaks of bones out of joint, a heart that is like wax, a mouth dried up like a potsherd, a tongue that sticks to his jaws, shriveled hands and feet. He is thin, so thin he can count all his bones. He is close to death.

He is afflicted, and, in his despair, he calls out to God, "Deliver my soul from the sword, / my life from the power of the dog! / Save me from the mouth of the lion!" (Ps. 22:20–21a).

In Psalm 18 there is another agonizing description of a worshiper caught in devastation. He is facing death, and he also cries out to God. The psalmist describes in symbolic and extraordinary language what happened when God heard his cry. The whole cosmos is at work in this mighty act. The earth reeled and rocked, the foundations of the mountains trembled and quaked. Smoke went up from God's nostrils, and glowing coals flamed forth from him. There was a thick darkness. God rode on a cherub and flew swiftly upon the wings of the wind. Hailstones and coals of fire broke through the clouds. And then the voice of the Lord was heard. Yahweh sent out arrows, flashed forth lightening. God laid bare the foundations of the earth.

This, for the psalmist, is a portrait of the moment of deliverance. "He reached down from on high, he took me; / he drew me out of mighty waters. / He delivered me from my strong enemy, / and from those who hated me; / for they were too mighty for me… / he delivered me, because he delighted in me" (Ps. 18:16–17, 19b). (This leads to complicated and thorny theological questions! Would God have delivered the psalmist if God did not "delight" in him?) Or, does God delight in everyone?

These are rendering portraits of persons who are oppressed by the enemy and who have known oppression. In Psalm 71 again the worshiper cries out. This is a worshiper who has known God all of his days: "Upon you I have leaned from my birth" (v. 6). Now, though older and with gray hair, the worshiper continues to ask for God to intervene into his life, to rescue him from those who seek to hurt him. His enemies say that God has forsaken him, and he cries out, "In you, O Lord, I take refuge; / let me never be put to shame. / In your righteousness deliver me…" (vv. 1–2a). It is God who rescues us from life's trials.

Not all prayers for deliverance are for one's self. In Psalm 82, the one crying out sees that there is injustice in the world. Observing the world around him, he sees that the wicked are far more prosperous than others; God seems to show them partiality. The psalmist cries out, "Give justice to the weak and the orphan; / maintain the right of the lowly and the destitute. / Rescue the weak and the needy; / deliver them from the hand of the wicked" (vv. 4–5). The one who is praying to God sees the despair and the grief of the oppressed and cries out on their behalf. He has witnessed God's care, and he is now the voice for the voiceless.

There are several Hebrew words translated as "to deliver" that paint the portrait of the one who delivers us.[3] One of them is also translated "to save" the one who delivers is the one who brings salvation. The deliverer is savior.

One of the primary deliverance stories is the recounting of God sending Moses back to Egypt to save the Israelites from the oppression of the mighty Pharaoh. The Israelites under the leadership of Moses left Egypt and began the journey toward a land they had never seen, never known. As they began the long and torturous journey, they set up camp between Migdol and the sea, just as Yahweh had told them. When Pharaoh found out that they had left, he regretted having let them go. He took the chariots and the officers over them, and began to pursue the Israelites, who had made a temporary home by the sea. The Israelites looked back and saw the Egyptians advancing on them. They were afraid. They cried out to Yahweh and to Moses. They were afraid that they would die.

The rest of the story is one of the most well-known Old Testament narratives. Popularized by film and painting, we hold in our minds the image of Moses stretching out his hand over the sea, the waves dividing to let the Israelites pass on to freedom. At the end of the story, the narrator says to us, "Thus the LORD saved [delivered] Israel that day" (Ex. 14:30). It is thought that the word for salvation is related to other words meaning "spacious" and "wide." There is in this notion a hopefulness that God can deliver us from what restricts and oppresses us. We are given room, a liberating space within which we can live our lives. The Old Testament holds that God actively participates in the life of the community and the individual; that God hears the cries of distress that arise from us, and that God is willing and desirous that we be given a full and wide berth to live out life abundantly.

Dew

I will heal their disloyalty; / I will love them freely, / for my anger has turned from them. / I will be like the dew to Israel; / he shall blossom like the lily, / he shall strike root like the forests of Lebanon. / His shoots shall spread out; / his beauty shall be like the olive tree, / and his fragrance like that of Lebanon.
Hosea 14:4–6

The Old Testament bears witness to a dynamic, challenging, sometimes waning relationship between the people and their God. The book of Judges recounts a cyclical history during which the people become unfaithful to God. They then find themselves in the most trying of circumstances and oppressed. They cry out to their God. God hears them and sends a judge to deliver them. For a while, the relationship is restored and renewed, until, almost inevitably, the people again distance themselves and become unfaithful. Their "on again, off again" relationship with God is described in many ways and the historical circumstances vary, but underneath it all is a story of a straying people.

Hosea paints for us a graphic image of these people. In words that he speaks on behalf of Yahweh, he says to the people, "Your love is like a morning cloud, / like the dew that goes away early" (6:4). The prophet has captured for us the essence of the people's straying. When you awake in the morning, there are very fine drops of water covering the grass. Sometimes they are not visible, but they can be felt if you walk barefoot across the lawn. There is moistness; dampness has settled during the night hours. Then, as the sun's rays begin to streak across the sky and the rays hit the morning dew, it disappears. It is gone. What shall I do with you? God asks. What shall I do? Your love is like the dew that goes away very early in the morning.

Later, Hosea, the master of metaphor, again uses this same image to describe the people's lack of allegiance to God, or perhaps their fate, because they have been unfaithful. The people are like the morning mist, the dew that goes away early. They are like chaff that swirls from the threshing floor. They are like smoke from a window (13:3). They are seen and then unseen. They are here and then they are gone—vanished, out of sight.

The wonder of metaphors is that they are flexible and multidimensional. Here is where the book of Hosea shows part of its genius. The people are like the dew because it goes away just as the people have gone away from their God—but God?

God is also like the dew. Not because God is fickle and goes away. God is like the dew because even the slightest amount of life-giving water can renew and restore. "I will heal their disloyalty; / I will love them freely, / for my anger has turned from them. / I will be like the dew to Israel; / he will blossom like the lily, / he shall strike root like the forests of Lebanon" (Hos. 14:4–5). In unparalleled words of grace and reconciliation, God will be like the dew. Even the smallest drops of water will recreate the people, and they will flourish like the finest of gardens, like a strong and mighty forest.

The "dew of heaven" is an important dimension of Israelite blessings. When the aging Isaac blesses his son Jacob (Gen. 27:28), he says, "May God give you of the dew of heaven, / and of the fatness of the earth, / and plenty of grain and wine." This is an agricultural blessing: may Jacob's crops always be bountiful. This is an important blessing in a region where crops are dependent upon rainfall and where the threat of drought always looms. This same dimension is seen in Moses' final blessing of the Israelites before he dies and before they cross over the Jordan River to continue their journey: "So Israel lives in safety, / untroubled is Jacob's abode / in a land of grain and wine, / where the heavens drop down dew" (Deut. 33:28). Again, the blessing is for fertile land washed with the waters that come down from the heavens.

The watered earth, the dew, is God's gift. That is dramatically seen in the wilderness wanderings when the Israelites are hungry and without food and without drink. The dew comes down in the morning, and when it fades away, the dry flaky substance is left on the ground. The substance is manna; it is the bread that Yahweh has miraculously provided for them. The manna nourishes and energizes and it enables the Israelites to keep on their journey.

God sends the dew of heaven to feed. God is like the dew of heaven because God nourishes us on our journey.

Eagle

You have seen what I did to the Egyptians, and how I bore you on eagles' wings and brought you to myself. Now therefore, if you obey my voice and keep my covenant, you shall be my treasured possession out of all the peoples. Exodus 19:4–5

And God said to Moses, "You have seen what I did to the Egyptians, and how I bore you on eagles' wings and brought you to myself." The Israelites had been brought through the Red Sea, the threat of the Egyptians safely behind them. They had been caught between the thunderous sounds of the chariots and Pharaoh's men behind them and the large, looming sea ahead. The sea opened and they passed through. It was, God was telling them, as if they had been picked up off the rumbling soil and carried high in the clouds to new life. They had been transported, rescued, delivered out of the trouble that seemingly could not be escaped. At least, there was no human way to survive. But it was God who miraculously delivered them through the water—as if they were on the wings of the eagle (Ex. 19:4-5).

God did not abandon them there. God sustained them in the desert land and in the wilderness. In the howling wasteland, God cared for them, and guarded them. "As an eagle stirs up its nest, / and hovers over its young; / as it spreads its wings, takes them up, / and bears them aloft on its pinions, / the Lord alone guided him [Israel]" (Deut. 32:11–12a). The song recorded in Deuteronomy 32 brings us this description of the wilderness wanderings. God is like the mother eagle looking over her precious young. She lifts them up and carries them along the way. She carries them on top of her wings to protect them from the hunters below.[4]

What a strange description of the wanderings in the wilderness! As one reads through Exodus, Leviticus, Numbers, and Deuteronomy, the described journey seems like anything but a comfortable flight on the back of the eagle. It seems like a long, slow journey filled with hunger and thirst, disappointment and despair, death and longing for times past. The picture painted of the mother eagle seems simply to be this: that God was always there with them. What they needed, God provided. When they were weary and faint, it was God who renewed their energy and allowed them to go on.

The Jewish rabbis were thinking about Exodus 19:4 ("How I bore you on eagles' wings..."). They thought about the ways that the eagle was different from other fowl and why it would be chosen to depict the God who would swoop down and carry the Israelites through their difficult journey. How is the eagle different? All other birds, they said, carry their young between their feet. They are afraid of the birds flying above them. But the eagle is mighty; the eagle is afraid only of humans—those who might shoot arrows at them. The eagle, then, carries its young on its wings, thinking that it would rather have the arrows from below hit its own self rather than its children.[5] Second Isaiah seemed to understand this exodus journey. God gives power to the faint, he said. God strengthens the powerless. "Those who wait for the LORD shall renew their strength, / they shall mount up with wings like eagles, / they shall run and not be weary, / they shall walk and not faint" (40:31).

This image of the eagle in flight is a reality and a hope. The eagles soaring high in the blue sky—it seems so effortless, so graceful, so uninhibited and unencumbered by scarred landscapes and divides. The eagle glides above them. God said to the people through Moses, "I bore you on eagles' wings and brought you to myself" (Ex. 19:4). Whatever tragedy or difficulty came to them on their journey, whatever happened that made them turn away from God, God was there. God was ready to swoop down and carry them up and bring them back to the place they belonged.

Enemy

For the enemy has pursued me, / crushing my life to the ground, / making me sit in darkness like those long dead. Psalm 143:3

When the ways of people please the LORD, / he causes even their enemies to be at peace with them. Proverbs 16:7

Do not rejoice when your enemies fall, / and do not let your heart be glad when they stumble. Proverbs 24:17

In Genesis 17 God makes a covenant with Abraham. God blesses him, saying that he will have offspring as numerous as the stars of heaven and the sand on the seashore. And...the offspring will possess the gate of the enemy. In the beginning scenes of the great historical drama of Abraham and his children, the text acknowledges that this great family and mighty nation will have enemies. There are no nations without enemies, and enemies are created in a multitude of ways and for different reasons. A nation can be perceived as an enemy because it is powerful and poses a constant threat to other nations less powerful or large. Or a nation can be an enemy because it has control over a resource that is desired or needed. Or a nation can be an enemy simply because the language spoken is "different" or because its people have a different color of skin stretched over their bones. Or perhaps there have been problems or skirmishes in the past, incidents that cannot be easily forgotten.

It is not surprising that the small nation of Israel, nestled at the edge of the Mediterranean Sea, had its enemies. It lay at the crossroads of mighty empires that needed clearance through its borders. Dwarfed by the empires around it, Israel and its leader turned to their God to help them survive. The Israelites had enemies in the wilderness, enemies when they took over the land, and national enemies as the kings took their places on the throne. There were enemies on every side.

In the Psalms there is a recurring and constant appeal to God to deliver the worshiper or the worshiper's community from the enemy. We are not always certain exactly who those enemies are. Sometimes they seem to be nations surrounding the small country of Israel. Sometimes the enemy seems to be sickness or those who persecute, taunt, oppress, and humiliate. The cries of the one in distress are piercing: "Deliver me, O my God! / For you strike all my enemies on the cheek..." (Ps. 3:7). "The LORD has heard my supplication; / the LORD accepts my prayer. / All my enemies shall be ashamed and struck with terror..." (Ps. 6:9–10a). "How long, O LORD? Will you forget me forever? / How long will you hide your face from me? / How long must I bear pain in my soul, and have sorrow in my heart all day long? / How long shall my enemy be exalted over me?" (Ps. 13:1–2). The worshiper cries out to God to help and expresses confidence that God will.

These quotations from the Psalms are troubling enough. The worshiper calls upon God to destroy the enemy and calls forth revenge upon them. Our ears at first cringe at these very honest exclamations, yet we recognize their humanness. We know that we have felt this way at times ourselves. It is important to remember that the Psalms are not describing how we should be. The Psalms mirror who and how we are. They are graphic portraits of the struggles and difficulties and challenges and cruelties of life. We have enemies. Sometimes we want to bring their demise. Rarely in our worship do we have such explicit cries of despair and anger targeted at those who despise or work against us. And, for some, it is the church who is the enemy—the church that will not welcome them, accept them, allow them positions of leadership.

These images are not as troubling, however, as the images from the book of Lamentations, where the narrator and the city of Jerusalem are not crying out to God because of their enemies. They are crying out to God, who *is* the enemy. "The Lord has become like an enemy; / he has destroyed Israel; / He has destroyed all its palaces, / laid in ruins its strongholds, / and multiplied in daughter Judah / mourning and lamentation" (Lam. 2:5).

The book of Lamentations is written as an elegy, a song of death. Daughter Zion, Jerusalem, has experienced immeasurable suffering. She sits lonely like a widow, crying bitterly in the night. Her majesty is gone, faded. She is now a mockery and all despise her. Over and again we hear that there is no one to comfort her. There is talk of her enemies (1:2, 5, 9, 16, 21; 2:3, 4, 5, 7, 16, 22). But who is the enemy? The imagery moves intricately back and forth. It is not clear if the enemy is just the foreign invader that demolished the city and its temple. Or is it God? Or both?[6]

The book of Lamentations leaves us with eerie and unsettling questions about defeat and devastation. Did these come from God? Or were these the rightful and natural consequences of the people's unfaithfulness? Did the people experience the devastation of the city of Jerusalem, the city they thought would never be destroyed, and attribute the devastation to God? Was that easier than thinking that their God was not powerful enough to save them?

How do we account for evil? How do we account for tragedies that we experience in our own lives? In our communities? What do these have to do with the God whom we worship?

Father

I have found my servant David; / with my holy oil I have anointed him; / my hand shall always remain with him; / my arm also shall strengthen him. / The enemy shall not outwit him, / the wicked shall not humble him. / I will crush his foes before him / and strike down those who hate him. / My faithfulness and steadfast love shall be with him; / and in my name his horn shall be exalted. / I will set his hand on the sea / and his right hand on the rivers. / He shall cry to me, "You are my Father, / my God, and the Rock of my salvation." Psalm 89:20–26

I suspect that if church members were asked to name the most commonly used metaphor for God in the Old Testament, many might say "Father." It is surprising to find that they would be wrong. God is given the name Father only a handful of times—in the law, the prophets and the writings *rarely* do we encounter the understanding of God as father.[7] That makes us wonder, then, when it was used, what did it signify? What related thoughts or images or feelings accompanied its usage? There are some clues for us.

In Deuteronomy 32 Moses is singing a song to the people. It's not a comforting song; it is not a love song, not a lullaby. It is a song that brings a harsh indictment to the people who have been delivered from Egypt and who are walking through the wilderness. As in other lawsuits, Moses calls upon the earth and the heavens to hear the words that he will be speaking. In contrast to the unfaithful people, Moses describes a God who has been constant and sure. "The Rock, his work is perfect, / and all his ways are just. / A faithful God, without deceit, / just and upright is he; / yet his degenerate children have dealt falsely with him, / a perverse and crooked generation" (Deut. 32:4–5). The singer draws a sharp contrast between the ways of the people and the ways of God. How could the people be unfaithful to a God who has always been faithful to them? How could they be foolish and senseless when their God is perfect and honest and just? The unbelieving singer of the song asks, "Is not he your father, who created you, / who made you and established you?" (v. 6). The God who is father is the one who gave them life, created and formed them.

In a communal lament, Isaiah also uses the metaphor of father for God. The worshiper recounts all the grace-filled deeds of Yahweh and names the many things that God has done for God's people (Isa. 63:7ff). God saved the people and redeemed them because God loved them. God lifted them up and carried them through all the trials and miseries of the days of old. But, as in Deuteronomy, Isaiah knows that in the face of the faithful God the people have been unfaithful. They rebelled and grieved God. Where is the God who once delivered their ancestors through the Red Sea? The people call to God to look down from the heavens and see them. They cry out for God's compassion. "For you are our father…" (63:16a).

The prophet calls out, "O that you would tear open the heavens and come down…" (Isa. 64.1a). The people are desperate for a sign of God's presence. They need reassurance that the God who delivered them in days past is still listening to them, watching out over them, caring for them. They think that God has hidden God's face. And yet…"O Lord, you are our Father, / we are clay, and you are our potter; / we are all the work of your hand. / Do not be exceedingly angry, O Lord, / and do not remember iniquity forever" (64:8–9).

In the end, for the Israelites to know God as father was to know the one who created them, just as the potter creates with clay. To know God as father was to know that God would acknowledge them and their plight. And to know God as father was to know that God would be compassionate and deliver them.[8]

Psalm 103 is a compelling testimony to God's amazing grace and to the perpetual and far-reaching ways that God's mercy extends out into the world. The psalmist begins by naming his need to give thanksgiving and to bless the Lord. The psalmist has this burning desire to express his gratitude because God forgives sin, heals diseases, redeems life, crowns us with steadfast love and mercy, gives good things, and renews. God works for justice for those who are oppressed. God is merciful and gracious and slow to anger and abounding in steadfast love. God's steadfast love is as high as the heavens over the earth. And it expands from the farthest reaches of east to west. God can move our transgressions that far away. This is a beautiful portrait of the God who forever seeks to restore, renew, and allow us the opportunity of ever new beginning. The psalmist caps this description by saying, "As a father has compassion for his children, / so the Lord has compassion for those who fear him" (v. 13).

For the psalmist the ultimate "picture" of a compassionate, grace-giving God is as Father.

These references leave us with interesting questions about the very scarce and limited use of the metaphor of "father" in the world of the ancient Israelites. The word brings forth a web of comforting images. Yet, with all the beauty that this metaphor potentially holds, there are complexities associated with its use. "God the father" has become more than a metaphor, a way of talking about one aspect of the nature of God. It has become a model or, we might say, idol that has created and reinforced patriarchal assumptions about the primacy of male over female, father over mother, man over wife. Throughout the centuries it has become the way not only to see part of the nature of God but also our relationships with one another. When our metaphors for deity are primarily masculine (father, king, husband, master), these images can form and fashion our living. If we forget that "God as father" is merely metaphor, we make it God's name. God as father can then be translated into "fathers are gods," and the world, our social lives, families, business lives, all become places where male comes first—where male attitudes and understanding define what is "normal."[9]

Father of Orphans

Wash yourselves; make yourselves clean; / remove the evil of your doings / from before my eyes; / cease to do evil, / learn to do good; / seek justice, rescue the oppressed, / defend the orphan, / plead for the widow. Isaiah 1:16–17

For if you truly amend your ways and your doings, if you truly act justly one with another, if you do not oppress the alien, the orphan, and the widow, or shed innocent blood in this place, and if you do not go after other gods to your own hurt, then I will dwell with you in this place, in the land that I gave of old to your ancestors forever and ever. Jeremiah 7:5–7

...you have been the helper of the orphan. Psalm 10:14d

We are accustomed to turning to the words recorded by the Old Testament prophets when we want to read about God's demand for righteousness and justice on the earth. We read the words of Micah 6:8, "What does the LORD require of you / but to do justice, and to love kindness, / and to walk humbly with your God?" Or, we consider the rousing words from Amos: "Let justice roll down like waters, /

and righteousness like an ever-flowing stream" (5:24). The prophets name clearly for us the realities of our living. It is the prophets who speak to us about protecting the most vulnerable among us. Often they tell us that practicing our rituals, or participating in extravagant worship, is not enough. God demands more. God demands right and just relationships among the people.

There is hidden in the Psalms, however, a gentler reminder that God is concerned about the poor and the oppressed. This message doesn't come in strident, urgent oracles delivered by fiery prophets. It comes in the prayers of those who have come to worship. The message is subtle and easy to miss. But it is there.

"But you do see! Indeed you note trouble and grief, / that you may take it into your hands; / the helpless commit themselves to you; / you have been the helper of the orphan" (Ps. 10:14). Through this naming of God, the praying one acknowledges that God sees the plight of those who have no power or authority in this world. Surely in ancient Israel the orphans were the most vulnerable and the ones looked down upon in the world. But God sees and God hears their cries.

God does even more. God loves these as a parent loves. "Father of orphans and protector of widows / is God in his holy habitation. / God gives the desolate a home to live in; / he leads out the prisoners to prosperity, / but the rebellious live in parched land" (Ps. 68:5–6). God gives them what they need. The orphan needs a parent, and the widow, who has no one to care for her or give her status in the community, needs a protector. God is those things. God calls us to be those things. That is how the quiet prayers of the worshiper and the prophetic proclamations work hand in hand. Both reveal that God cares for those who are often ignored. Both reveal that God needs us to notice and provide for them.

This God who is the "father of the fatherless" longs for each person created in God's image to be loved and cared for. But God is interested in more. God is interested in working toward a just world where the systems that oppress and devalue and diminish and silence are dismantled and disrupted. God loves the orphan *and* God wants to "pluck up" those things in the world that keep the orphan's demise in place. We see that clearly in Psalm 68 where God is on a rampage. Just as wax melts before the fire, so God intends to destroy and scatter all who oppress the children God loves.

Fire

*For the L*ORD* your God is a devouring fire, a jealous God.*
Deuteronomy 4:24

A spark...a flame...a burning bush. And the exodus from Egypt began (Ex. 3). The angel of God appeared in the wilderness to Moses. The bush was blazing, but not consumed. And Moses turned aside to see this great thing that was happening. The fire had done its magic; it had captured the attention of the shepherd. Then God called to Moses from the flame. He called his name—two times: "Moses, Moses!" And Moses answered, "Here I am" (v. 4). And God told him to take the sandals from his feet because the place of the burning fire was holy. Moses hid his face because he was afraid to see God.

And the LORD said:

> I have observed the misery of my people who are in Egypt; I have heard their cry on account of their taskmasters. Indeed, I know their sufferings, and I have come down to deliver them from the Egyptians, and to bring them up out of that land to a good and broad land, a land flowing with milk and honey... (Ex. 3:7—8)

Moses became the deliverer for the Israelites in Egypt. Facing the great Pharaoh and demonstrating the power of God, Moses convinced the people to leave with him. They began their journey through the wilderness on the way to the Red Sea. And as they walked through this unknown land, God was with them. God appeared as a pillar of cloud by day, to lead them along the way. And God appeared as a pillar of fire by night, to give them light, so that they could keep traveling; so that they could travel safely; so that they could make it to the Sea.

The Israelites cross through the sea that Moses had parted. They face a wilderness, wide and long. They had never been there before. Neither had they seen the land of their destination and dreams. The journey was hard. Was this better than slavery in Egypt? They were not sure. Was God with them as God had promised? Where was the water they needed? Where was the food they needed so that they would survive? They couldn't go back; the great sea was now a giant barrier behind them. And they felt at times they couldn't go forward. *Was the God who accompanied them the God of their expectations? Is ours?*

They came upon the mountain where God would give them the law. God spoke out of the fire, the cloud, and the thick darkness. God wrote on two tablets of stone and gave them to Moses. When the community heard the voice coming out of the darkness, while the mountain was burning with fire, they came to Moses and said, "Look, the LORD our God has shown us his glory and greatness, and we have heard his voice out of the fire. Today we have seen that God may speak to someone and the person may still live" (Deut. 5:22–25).

The fire is an important part of the exodus story. It called Moses, guided the Israelites on their journey, and gave forth the law that would govern the people forever.

The story is not over at Sinai. The Israelites continue their journey, and in the book of Deuteronomy we find them poised on the edge of the river Jordan, ready to enter into the new land. Moses will not be allowed to go with them and so we find in Deuteronomy his last words to the community. Last words are important; Moses is giving his guidance and counsel to them. There are so many things he wants them to remember; he wants the best for their future. He wants them to be faithful to the God who has brought them through the wilderness. He wants them to be true to their covenant.

"Be careful to remember," is the word of Moses to the community with which he has traveled. Moses wants them *not* to be lured or seduced by other gods or by idols, because he believes that the Israelite's one God is the source of their hope and their prosperity. Moses says to them, "The LORD your God is a devouring fire, a jealous God" (Deut 4:24). The God who has cared for them and stayed with them expects the same in return. God demands loyalty and faithfulness.

God as fire—this is a God who holds expectations for individuals and community. God is like a fire that burns away that which is unhelpful for our living so that what is left is refined and is pure. In the prophets God is like a fire that burns away injustice so that those who are oppressed can find new and productive ways of living.

Fortress

David spoke to the Lord the words of this song on the day when the Lord delivered him from the hand of all his enemies, and from the hand of Saul. He said:

The Lord is my rock, my fortress, and my deliverer, / my God, my rock in whom I take refuge, / my shield and the horn of my salvation, / my stronghold and my refuge, / my savior; you save me from violence. / I call upon the Lord, who is worthy to be praised, / and I am saved from my enemies. 2 Samuel 22:1–4

"Fortress"…it is often found hidden away in a long list of metaphors that worshipers use in the Psalms to address God. In Psalm 18, for instance, the worshiper (named as David) sang a song on the day he was delivered from his enemy. The song is addressed to Yahweh, who is strength, rock, fortress, deliverer, rock, refuge, shield, salvation, and stronghold. It is as if one word, one name, is not enough to express the joy and gratitude of the one who has faced adversity and persevered.

The psalm continues, and the singer describes how he was in a dangerous place, very close to death. He cried to God for help. God heard him and delivered. The earth, the whole cosmos groaned, reeled, and rocked. The mountains quaked. God reached down and took the one who was afraid, who was staring death in the eyes. God drew him out of the mighty waters and delivered him from the enemy.

As in Psalm 18, the metaphor "fortress" is often used in combination with two other metaphors—"rock" and "refuge." In Psalm 31, for instance, notice how the three are used in combination with each other and, in this instance, even repeated, so the reader becomes fully aware that the three work in relationship with each other: "Incline your ear to me; / rescue me speedily. / Be a rock of refuge for me, / a strong fortress to save me" (v. 2). "You are indeed my rock and my fortress; / for your name's sake lead me and guide me, / take me out of the net that is hidden for me, / for you are my refuge" (v. 3). Also read Psalms 71, 91, and 144, where the words *fortress, rock,* and *refuge* form a web of meaning.

Fortress, then, is two things. First it is related to rock. It is strong, firm, lasting, and unwavering. In the Psalms, the psalmist relies on God because he is being plagued, tortured, or humiliated by the enemy. The psalmist cries out to God, and he can depend on God's presence to sustain him.

This is the understanding that is found in the Martin Luther hymn "A Mighty Fortress is our God." The hymn paints the picture of a world that threatens to undo our living, a world that brings challenges and fear. It is through God's power that we can prevail over all that the world brings to us.

Fortress in the Psalms is also related to refuge. When being besieged by enemies, or by life itself, the fortress is the place that protects. It is the place within which one can rest, breathe, and replenish. It is the place where one feels secure.

God is the fortress—the place the psalmist could go for safety and certainty. The place that is stronger than any threat or any violence.

Friend

Thus the LORD used to speak to Moses face to face, as one speaks to a friend. Exodus 33:11a

It is a picture of solemn worship. Moses and the people are traveling through the wilderness. As they travel the "tent of meeting" goes with them. The Israelites had a longing to live in the presence of the speaking God. They constructed the tent, or the tabernacle, as they traveled from Egypt to Canaan. Once God had spoken to the Israelites to give them the Law, the tent was constructed. The tent was the locus of God's speaking presence. Through voice, there was a disclosure of God's purpose. It was a meeting place—not a monument to God, but the place that could be filled with the presence of a God in dialogue with humanity. In its darkness the tent provided Moses with privacy and isolation for this conversation.

The tent of meeting was pitched outside the camp. When Moses went out to the tent, all the people would rise and stand at the entrances of their own tents. What would Yahweh say to Moses? What kinds of instruction, or what word, did God have for them? Moses entered the tent. A pillar of cloud, signaling the presence of God, descended and remained there at the door to the tent. The people bowed down. And then, Yahweh talked with Moses face to face, as a person speaks to a friend.

This is a relational God, active and present with the Israelites on their journey. When God is understood as relational, revelation is mutual. There is giving and receiving. There is divine/human dialogue with questions and answers, objections and counter-statements, give and take, interacting tension between God and person. To hear God's voice is sometimes like hearing the voice of a friend, a friend who stays face to face. God is a friend who stays present with no pretense.

God Almighty/*El Shaddai*

The Almighty [Shaddai]—we cannot find him; / he is great in power and justice, / and abundant righteousness he will not violate. / Therefore mortals fear him; / he does not regard any who are wise in their own conceit. Job 37:23–24

In the book of Ruth, Naomi cries out. The Almighty has dealt very bitterly with her, and she is afflicted. She is crying out against a very powerful God—one who, she believes, has caused her devastation and despair. It is also a favorite name for God in the book of Job—*El Shaddai,* God Almighty.

We know already that *El* is a name for God. It means the great or powerful or mighty one. But what about *El Shaddai*? When the Greeks translated the Hebrew Bible into their own language, they translated *Shaddai* as "all sufficient." It is interesting that the Hebrew noun *shad* is always translated "breast." Much in the same way that a mother's breast is "sufficient" for her infant child, God is sufficient for God's people. *El Shaddai* is the God of blessing, the God of sustenance, sufficiency, and nourishment.[10]

As the book of Genesis is coming to a close, Jacob blesses his sons, saying:

> Joseph is a fruitful bough, / a fruitful bough by a spring; / his branches run over the wall. / The archers fiercely attacked him; / they shot at him and pressed him hard. / Yet his bow remained taut, / and his arms were made agile / by the hands of the Mighty One of Jacob, / by the name of the Shepherd, the Rock of Israel, / by the God [*El*] of your father, who will help you, / by the Almighty [*Shaddai*] who will bless you / with the blessings of heaven above, / blessings of the deep that lies beneath, / blessing of the breasts and of the womb. (Gen. 49:22—25)

Here it is clear. God, *El*, is the one who helps Israel in the time of need. But *El Shaddai* is the all-sufficient one, the mother for the nursing child, who gives us what we need, all we need, and showers blessings upon us. This name for God occurs several times in Genesis and is associated with times of blessing and covenant making. In 17:1–2, the writer of Genesis describes an encounter between Abram, who is ninety-nine years old, and Yahweh: "I am [*El Shaddai*]; walk before me, and be blameless. And I will make my covenant between me and you, and will make you exceedingly numerous." *El Shaddai* promises—to this very old man—descendants without number. With this promise comes a change in Abram's name to Abraham, because he will be blessed with offspring.

In Genesis 28:3, Isaac blesses his son Jacob and sends him away to find his bride from the house of Laban. "May [*El Shaddai*] bless you and make you fruitful and numerous, that you may become a company of peoples." Again, here the blessing is one of many descendants.

Genesis 35:11 recounts the story of God's appearance to Jacob; God says to him that his name is changed. Jacob's name is now Israel. God says to him, "I am [*El Shaddai*]; be fruitful and multiply;

a nation and a company of nations shall come from you, and kings shall spring from you." God promises Jacob descendants and the land that has been promised to his father and grandfather.

The name *El Shaddai* appears also in Israel's blessing on his sons as they go down to Egypt to buy food and there they encounter their brother Joseph. Again in 48:3, Jacob recalls for Joseph the blessing that was once given to him, "[*El Shaddai*] appeared to me at Luz in the land of Canaan and he blessed me, and said to me, 'I am going to make you fruitful and increase your numbers; I will make you a company of peoples, and will give this land to your offspring after you for a perpetual holding.'"

This name for God is closely associated with the blessing for numerous descendants and offspring without number. It is interesting, then, that *El Shaddai* could be associated with the words for breast and thus symbolizes the God who brings and then nurtures those in the future who are born into the covenant community. God will sustain them.

El Shaddai is also thought to mean "God, one of the Mountain," a reflection that this God is associated with high places, places closer to the heavens, places that are divine.

Healer

Praise the Lord! / How good it is to sing praises to our God; / for he is gracious, and a song of praise is fitting. / The Lord builds up Jerusalem; / he gathers the outcasts of Israel. / He heals the brokenhearted, / and binds up their wounds. Psalm 147:1–3

It is to a healing God that the psalmists often prayed. They had a deep and abiding understanding of a God who could somehow touch their lives, perhaps bring relief from pain, from disease, from the profound ache that comes from being ostracized. God could bring comfort to the lonely and the outcast. Those with broken hearts? God would heal them. The cries from the worshipers are piercing: "O Lord, do not rebuke me in your anger, / or discipline me in your wrath. / Be gracious to me, O Lord, for I am languishing; / O Lord, heal me, for my bones are shaking with terror" (Ps. 6:1–2). The one who speaks is worried that death is imminent. He is weary from moaning, and every night he floods his bed with tears; his eyes waste away because of grief. His enemies overwhelm him, and he is afraid.

The psalmist in Psalm 6 wants healing from grave illness. In Psalm 41, the psalmist says, "As for me, I said, 'O LORD, be gracious to me; / heal me, for I have sinned against you'" (v. 4). The prayer is asking God to heal the petitioner from his sin. Healing is associated with forgiveness. His enemies whisper empty words about him; they imagine the worst for him. Even his bosom friend, the person in whom he most trusted, who ate of his bread, has turned against him. The psalmist wants healing from betrayal and breach of trust. The psalmist wants to be upheld and be victorious in the face of the onslaught against him. God could bring healing to individuals; that is clearly demonstrated in the Psalms. But in the prophets, healing is generally a spiritual kind of healing for nations, rather than a physical healing for an individual. God could also heal communities. It was God who could heal the breaches that scarred the earth's landscape. In Isaiah 58 there is a potent rendering of what the earth's healing would look like. God the healer calls upon the covenant people to do healing work. God laments the empty rituals of the people. Those who were fasting were, at the same time, seeking their own pleasure and oppressing those who worked for them. There was violence. This was not a fast of God's choosing:

> Is not this the fast that I choose: / to loose the bonds of injustice, / to undo the thongs of the yoke, / to let the oppressed go free, / and to break every yoke? / Is it not to share your bread with the hungry, / and bring the homeless poor into your house; / when you see the naked, to cover them, / and not to hide yourself from your own kin? (Isa. 58:6—7)

God was calling the people to a healing that comes from the rigorous pursuit of justice, and from recognizing the plight of the poor. It is then that the light breaks forth, and healing springs up quickly. This is a communal healing. It comes from the recognition that we are "in this together." We are healed only when we *all* know healing. God brought healing to communities through the restoration of relationships, the rebuilding of a city, forgiveness, and the giving of renewed prosperity and joy.

The prophet Jeremiah renders a harsh indictment of the religious leadership of his day. He talks about the priests and prophets who look for unjust gain. They deal in falsehoods and not in truths: "They have treated the wound of my people carelessly, / saying, "Peace, peace," when there is no peace" (8:11). To "heal lightly" is to bring words of comfort instead of challenge. It is to bring words that whitewash the realities of the peoples' living, to bring words that wrongly imply that the people are engaged in healthy and righteous ways. Jeremiah is different. He clearly understands the demise of the community, and the ways of the people grieve Jeremiah and the God who called him: "My joy is gone, grief is upon me, / my heart is sick" (v. 18). There is a weeping, a sense of dismay, and there is mourning.

Helper

But you, O Lord, do not be far away! / O my help, come quickly to my aid! Psalm 22:19

Our soul waits for the Lord; / he is our help and shield. Psalm 33:20

I lift up my eyes to the hills— / from where will my help come? / My help comes from the Lord, / who made heaven and earth. Psalm 121:1–2

It is not as troubling as the image of a warrior. It is not as beautiful as the image of the dawn. It is not as powerful as fortress, and not as provocative as a woman giving birth. It is God as helper. Sometimes we think of "helper" as someone second rate, less educated, inferior, a servant—someone who leaves the real work, thinking, and doing to others. The helper only assists. But the cries from the worshipers in the Psalms seem to indicate something more vital and urgent than that. They cry out to God for help. In Psalm 38, the one crying out is in physical distress. He has no soundness in his flesh, no health in his bones. This, he believes, is because of his sin. His "wounds grow foul and fester / because of [his] foolishness" (v. 5). He is groaning not simply because of the burning in his loins but because of the tumult in his heart. He is penitent, remorseful. And, as his strength fails him, he knows where he can put his trust. "Do not forsake me, O LORD; / O my God, do not be far from me; / make haste to help me..." (v. 21).

It is this kind of profound "being with" and support and aid that Second Isaiah assures the community will come from God. God says through the prophet, "Do not fear, / I will help you" (41:13, 14). The helper is the one with strength. The helper is the one who provides courage. The helper is vital to life continued, to abundant living. And thus we sing, "O God, our help in ages past, our hope for years to come..."[11]

The helper, then, is not an assistant, a subordinate or an inferior. The Hebrew word translated helper carries no such meaning. The word is significant and vital. The helper is essential, fundamentally the source of strength and hope.

Interestingly, this Hebrew word for "helper" is also used in the second creation story. God had created Adam from the dust of the ground. And then God created a helper for him. The helper was Eve. For generations, of course, this word for helper has been used to justify the subjugation of women, who have been rendered and treated as second class. But the word for helper, most often used to describe God, is used here to glorify Eve's importance in providing companionship for the first human created. The female is created "corresponding" to the male, the writer of the creation story is careful to say. This relationship between male and female is to be mutual. It is to be equal.[12]

Hiding Place

Then I acknowledged my sin to you, / and I did not hide my iniquity; / I said, "I will confess my transgressions to the LORD," / and you forgave the guilt of my sin. / Therefore let all who are faithful / offer prayer to you; / at a time of distress, the rush of mighty waters / shall not reach them. / You are a hiding place for me; / you preserve me from trouble; / you surround me with glad cries of deliverance. Psalm 32:5–7

"Hiding place"—the term means hidden, covert, or secret. In Psalm 31 the worshiper needs to be hidden from those who have contentious tongues, those who are speaking slanderous words. In Psalm 32 the worshiper needs to be hidden from the rush of mighty waters that threaten to wash him away and take his life. And in Psalm 119 the worshiper needs to be hidden from the evildoers of the world who try to persuade him to stray from the law. He needs a hiding place so that they cannot find him (v. 114). His steadfast hope is that he can continue to keep God's commandments and live according to God's promise because he knows that in these things abundant life is found.

The psalmist's prayer is that his hope and trust in God will not one day bring him shame. His hiding place is God's word. He is wed to it; he will honor and love it. The statues of God will keep him safe; he does what is just and right. And he hopes that if he "hides" in God's word, God will provide him a hiding place from his enemy and oppressor.

God will save him from humiliation, defeat, or shame. This understanding is brought to music through the hymn "You Are My Hiding Place."[13] In it, the singer gives praise to God. When she is afraid, God sings a song of deliverance. This "Hiding Place God" is the place where the weak go and find strength. This is the place, this is the one who can be trusted.

Holy One

I will also praise you with the harp / for your faithfulness, O my God; / I will sing praises to you with the lyre, / O Holy One of Israel. Psalm 71:22

In the sixth chapter of Isaiah we read about the call of the prophet. He is standing in the temple in the year that King Uzziah died. He sees Yahweh sitting on a throne, high and lofty. Seraphs attend Yahweh, each one having six wings. One calls to another and says, "Holy, holy, holy is the LORD of hosts; / the whole earth is full of his glory" (Isa. 6:3). The vision is filled with the temple's shaking foundations and with smoke, each adding to the mystery. The prophet calls out, "Woe is me! I am lost, for I am a man of unclean lips, and I live among a people of unclean lips; yet my eyes have seen the King, the Lord of hosts!" (v. 5).

Holy in the Old Testament means that which is separate from that which is common. Holy means awesome. It means to have a character that is good, without evil or sin. It means, in a sense, to be "connected" with the Divine. It is no wonder, then, that the prophet, sensing this One who is holy, comes suddenly to realize and verbalize his own inadequacies and uncleanness. "Woe is me!" In fact, Isaiah of Jerusalem comes to realize not only his own sinfulness but also that of his community as well. He comes to recognize these realities when he gets a glimpse of the true nature and character of God. We sing about this kind of God when we sing: Holy, holy, holy, Lord God Almighty!

> Early in the morning our song shall rise to thee...
> cherubim and seraphim falling down before thee...
> perfect in power, in love, and purity.[14]

Throughout Isaiah and also in the Psalms, God is frequently referred to as the Holy One of Israel:

> Shout aloud and sing for joy, O royal Zion, / for great in your midst is the holy one of Israel. (Isa. 12:6)

> For thus said the Lord God, the Holy One of Israel: / In returning and rest you shall be saved; / in quietness and in trust shall be your strength. (Isa. 30:15)

> To whom then will you compare me, / or who is my equal? says the Holy One. (Isa. 40:25)

> For thus says the high and lofty one / who inhabits eternity, whose name is Holy: / I dwell in the high and holy place, / and also with those who are contrite and humble in spirit. (Isa. 57:15)

God is holy and apart from Israel. Yet God is also in their midst. God is high and lofty and holy, yet dwells with those who are humble. This is a God who teaches strength in quietness; a God of otherness and "with-ness," of transcendence and immanence; a God of paradox.

In the hymn "Holy, Holy, Holy!" we sing about this holy God who is merciful, mighty, in three persons, ever living, hidden from sinful eyes, unequaled, and perfect in power, love, and purity.[15]

Hunter

Ephraim has become like a dove, / silly and without sense; / they call upon Egypt, they go to Assyria. / As they go, I will cast my net over them; / I will bring them down like birds of the air...
Hosea 7:11–12a

In Psalm 10, the psalmist is lamenting to God. The wicked are persecuting the poor; they have devised schemes for them. They catch and trap them. The wicked, those who are greedy for their own gain, are filled with pride. They think that God will not see them, will not be aware of the ways they are treating the poor. Some of them wrongfully believe that there is no God. The wicked believe that they will never encounter adversity.

The psalmist describes the activities of the wicked. They speak words of cursing, and practice deceit and oppression, mischief and iniquity. They sit in the villages, and they hide there so that they can murder the innocent. They watch for the helpless, lurk in secret, seize the poor and drag them into the net. They stoop. They crouch, and they say, "God will never see." The psalmist is convinced, however, that God does see and that God will move to deliver the oppressed from those who overpower them.

Often in the Psalms the one who is being oppressed describes the powerful enemy as the one who throws out the net to catch him. (See Psalms 10:9; 31:4; 35:7; 57:6; 140:5.) The hope of the oppressed one is that the wicked will be caught in their own traps and that, eventually, the most vulnerable will be victorious.

It is interesting, then, that Hosea would use this image of the hunter, the one who seeks out prey with nets to catch them, to describe God. Hosea describes a people unfaithful to God. From the stirring first chapters where we witness the trials of Hosea and his unfaithful wife Gomer, through to the end, Hosea names the people of Israel as fickle and disloyal to Yahweh. The people go this way and that. They go to Egypt for help. They go to Assyria for help. They are like a dove, silly and without sense (7:11–12).

I will gather them, God says, and as they are running about, to and fro, I will throw my net over them like a hunter catches its prey. I will catch them like a hunter catches birds that fly through the air. I will discipline them because they have strayed and rebelled against me.

God will forcefully catch the people and stop their running about. They do not have an honest relationship with God; they do not cry to God from their hearts. Even though God has been with them, trained and educated and strengthened them, they turn away for things that really do not profit. They have misplaced priorities. They make bad investments in things that, in the long run, do not satisfy. They worship other gods. That is a violation of the covenant, and God is not pleased. It breaks God's heart. God the hunter will find them and claim them as God's own.

Husband

Do not fear, for you will not be ashamed; / do not be discouraged, for you will not suffer disgrace; / for you will forget the shame of your youth, / and the disgrace of your widowhood you will remember no more. / For your Maker is your husband, / the LORD of hosts is his name; / the Holy One of Israel is your Redeemer, / the God of the whole earth he is called. / For the LORD has called you / like a wife forsaken and grieved in spirit, / like the wife of a man's youth when she is cast off, / says your God. / For a brief moment I abandoned you, / but with great compassion I will gather you. / In overflowing wrath for a moment / I hid my face from you, / but with everlasting love I will have compassion on you, / says the LORD, your Redeemer. Isaiah 54:4–8

The above quotation from Second Isaiah is a troubling one. A family drama is played out before our eyes. Yahweh is husband;

Jerusalem is wife. She has been devastated and destroyed by the enemy. This is a song of restoration. The prophet promises that Jerusalem's disgrace and shame, her times of suffering and discouragement, are over. It is an apology, of sorts. It is an apology from God. It is also a confession: "For a brief moment I abandoned you, / but with great compassion I will gather you. / In overflowing wrath...I hid..., / but with everlasting love I will have compassion on you." The wife does not answer.

In the beginning chapters of Jeremiah, Yahweh is the husband. He is angry, jealous, petty, and abusive.[16] The husband is broken-hearted and abandoned, surprised by the failure of the marital relationship with Israel. He thinks that he has done everything possible to insure success and to make the marriage flourish.

The wife's infidelity is presented in the most shameful way possible. The broken marriage relationship is used to describe symbolically the history of Yahweh's relationship with Judah. The highly emotional language of the husband, his nostalgia, anger, and jealousy, would help gain the empathy of the readers (males) by bringing them to the side of the husband who was betrayed.[17]

This same scenario is played out for us in the first chapters of Hosea. These chapters are an extended metaphor. They draw a picture and, at the same time, they tell a story. It is a story about Hosea and his wife, Gomer.

God calls to Hosea and tells him to marry a wife of "whoredom," a wife who symbolizes the unfaithfulness of God's covenant people. Hosea does, and he and Gomer give birth to three children—Jezreel (God sows), Lo-ruhamah (No pity), and Lo-ammi (Not my people). The children's names symbolize the urgent plight of the people. God is ready to "call it quits." God will not show pity on them again. The covenant relationship will finally be broken. The familiar slogan that defined the essence of the covenant living, "I am your God; you are my people," will no longer be true. What was will be severed, finished.

The rage of Yahweh is evident. Yahweh pleads with the children to talk to their mother: "Tell her to be faithful, to put away her whoring and adultery. She has been unfaithful to me." And then Yahweh lists three consequences for her behavior:

Therefore I will hedge up her way with thorns; / and I will build a wall against her, / so that she cannot...pursue her lovers. (2:6–7a)

Therefore I will take back / my grain in its time, / and my wine in its season; / and I will take away my wool and my flax, / which were to cover her nakedness. (2:9) (emphasis added)

Therefore...

What could be next? we wonder. What is the third "therefore"? What kind of punishment does Yahweh have in store for his spouse? Will the third "therefore" be more drastic, more devastating, more destructive? It is not what we expect.

Therefore, I will now allure her, / and bring her into the wilderness, / and speak tenderly to her...

I will take you for my wife forever. (2:14, 19a)

In this story, God's everlasting love trumps God's anger. The relationship is once again restored. Yet, it is a troubling story. It plays out a family drama all too common. The angry spouse apologizes, makes a pledge never to be angry again. We have to ask how the troubling images of God as an abusive husband—one who abandons, punishes, and sexually abuses his spouse—have prompted or justified abuse toward women in our own world. We must address these texts that directly or subtly reinforce violence and speak out against them.

Judge

But the Lord sits enthroned forever, / he has established his throne for judgment. / He judges the world with righteousness; / he judges the peoples with equity. Psalm 9:7–8

The psalmist says that the nations should be glad and even should sing for joy because God judges the earth with equity. Usually impending judgment does not bring exclamations of gratitude and thanksgiving! But, perhaps, that is because we don't really understand or acknowledge the meanings of judgment, and thus justice, in the Old Testament. We ask, "Why is judgment necessary?"

Not surprisingly, the word translated "justice" grows out of a legal context. The word can mean court case or the process of administering the law. It can also mean the verdict that is delivered in a certain case, or the law in its abstract sense. At its root, then, the words mean judging in accordance with the law. God is the judge who executes justice and law. God is the mighty and powerful judge who is impartial and who cannot be deflected from the course of executing judgment. God executes justice for the fatherless and widows, and God loves strangers by giving them food. God's insistence that there be justice is motivated by concern for the weak and the oppressed. God judges the oppressor. God's insistence on justice is mandated by the concern for those to whom justice is denied.

It is, then, the recurring accusation of the prophets that the people do not champion the cause of the poor and the oppressed, that the denial of justice to the orphan and the needy is what brings on the anger of God. God's anger has, as its source, compassion for those who, by the denial of justice, carry the burden of our sinfulness: "He will judge the world with righteousness" (Ps. 98:9). There is a relationship between being a judge and restoring righteousness— right relationships between God and people and people with each other. A psalmist cries out, "'Give justice to the weak and the orphan;/ maintain the right of the lowly and the destitute. / Rescue the weak and the needy; deliver them from the hand of the wicked.'...Rise up, O God, judge the earth" (Ps. 82:3–4, 8a).

There is a call from many lamenters in the Psalms; they cry out for God to judge them. This is often translated "Vindicate me!" (26:1, 35:24; 43:1) These are cries from the oppressed, those who are being tormented by their enemies and evildoers. They want God to judge the earth, for the exploited and the vulnerable to find equity, and for the oppressors to know God's disapproval.

Leopard, Lion, Mother Bear

So I will become like a lion to them, / like a leopard I will lurk beside the way. Hosea 13:7

In Hosea the prophet brings strong indictments against the people who have been idolatrous and unfaithful to their God. Woven throughout these harsh accusations are words of comfort, hope, and restoration. These words are found, for instance, in chapters 2, 11, and in the book's closing verses. Once the words of restoration are spoken, however, the prophet returns to his rampage against the nation.

Chapter 13 is one of the texts that speak of God's relentless judgment against the people. The people who make and sacrifice to idols made of silver are described as people who will not long survive. Hosea uses a list of metaphors to describe them. They are like the morning mist and the dew that goes away early in the morning, like chaff that blows away from the threshing floor, and like the smoke that is seen and then disappears as it makes its way out the window (v. 3). The future of the people is uncertain. Perhaps soon they will no longer exist; like the mist, the dew, the chaff, and the smoke, they will no longer be seen, no longer be visible to the world around them.

God continues by outlining the things God has done for Israel. God led them out of the slavery in Egypt. God led them through the wilderness. And yet the people, as they had done before, *forgot* the God who had walked with them. Again they had forgotten. And so...

Hosea then uses a triad of animal images to describe God's response to the unfaithful people who have been the recipients of God's steadfast love and care:

> So I will become like a lion to them, / like a leopard I will lurk beside the way. / I will fall upon them like a bear robbed of her cubs, / and will tear open the covering of their heart; / there I will devour them like a lion, / as a wild animal would mangle them. (13:7–8)

It is not the leopard that is so troubling in Hosea 13:7. It is the idea of a *lurking* leopard. Is God like one who lies secretly in wait, hiding from the prey? Perhaps this is close to the meaning Hosea intends. The leopard, according to the rendering of the Hebrew verb, is watching and observing. The leopard is looking, noticing, watching, and waiting; God is waiting because the people God has cared for and loved have forgotten God.

Further threats and warnings follow this leopard, bear, and lion sequence. Then, in Chapter 14, there is an urgent appeal to Israel to return to Yahweh. The prophet who has reprimanded them begs them to repent. Hosea tells them what to say! They will no longer worship that which they have made with their hands. And then comes the assurance of forgiveness from the God who will heal them, love them, turn anger away from them. In the book of Hosea, this restoration is left as the final, lingering word.

Light

Do not rejoice over me, O my enemy; / when I fall, I shall rise; / when I sit in darkness, / the LORD will be a light to me.
Micah 7:8

Light is sweet, and it is pleasant for the eyes to see the sun.
Ecclesiastes 11:7

"The LORD bless you and keep you; / the LORD make his face to shine [to bring light] upon you, and be gracious to you; / the LORD lift up his countenance upon you, and give you peace" (Num. 6:24–26). This benediction is well known in Christian and Jewish communities alike. The importance of this blessing and its ancient character is witnessed by an archeological discovery in Jerusalem. This benediction was found inscribed on two silver cylinders dated 600 B.C.E. These cylinders are the earliest known fragments of any biblical texts and predate the Dead Sea Scrolls by four hundred years.[18]

The benediction asks for God to shine light on the one being blessed and for God to lift God's face and bless the community. The gift is summed up in the final word of the blessing—*shalom*. This is the ultimate gift: a gift of health, prosperity, friendship, well-being, justice, and salvation. These are the things that make life possible and full. These are the result of God's "keeping" us (v. 24).

This is the constant petition of the psalmists. They want, in their day-to-day living and in their day-to-day struggling, for God's face to shine upon them. "Let your face shine upon your servant" (Ps. 31:16). In Psalm 80, this same petition is repeated as if the request is urgent, and the worshiper demands God's attention (vv. 3, 7; see also 119:135). There are many, many consequences of God's being a light in our lives.

When God is light, one need not fear (Ps. 27:1). The psalmist walks in a world of shadow and discomfort. There are enemies and foes; they are encamped against him. His heart pounds with anxiety because he is in danger. Yet, even in the midst of the chaos of anxiety and apprehension, the light of God shines. With God as his "stronghold," he asks, "Of whom shall I be afraid?"

When God is light, we ourselves can see hope for the future (Ps. 36:9). The psalmist knows of God's steadfast love and salvation. God is the fountain, the source, of all of life. Because God's light is shining around us, it shines on us and in us and through us.

When God is light, God shines through our works of justice (Ps. 37:6). If we are trustworthy, God will act through us. We become God's light in the world; it will be as if the world is as light as the noonday.

When God is light, we see truth (Ps. 43:3). When God sends God's light out to us, we are led to the truth. We are led to the altar of God, which is our hope. "Why are you cast down, O my soul, / and why are you disquieted within me? / Hope in God; for I shall again praise him, / my help and my God" (v. 5).

When God is light, the path is made clear (Ps. 56:13). When we walk in God's light we are delivered from wandering, from failing, from following pathways that lead only to destruction and death.

Maggots/Moth/Rottenness

You chastise mortals / in punishment for sin, / consuming like a moth what is dear to them; / surely everyone is a mere breath.
Psalm 39:11

Hosea is the master of metaphor. In striking and dramatic imagery, the prophet describes the unfaithfulness of the people and the fury of God's response to them.

To the people, God says through Hosea, "Your love is like a morning cloud, / like the dew that goes away early" (6:4b). The people have once loved God, but their love is not permanent; it is not everlasting. God cannot depend upon it. Like the fog that shrouds the earth at sunrise, their love melts away with the morning sun.

And like the dew that covers the grass at dawn, their love quickly disappears.

Because the people are fickle and untrustworthy, God is angry. The people have worshiped other gods. The Northern Kingdom of Ephraim and the Southern Kingdom of Judah have put faith in other gods, other nations, and other alliances. "Therefore I am like maggots to Ephraim, / and like rottenness to the house of Judah" (5:12).

God is like maggots (or moths)? God is like rottenness? These are not the kinds of images of God that are comfortable and familiar to many of us. They show anger. They speak of judgment and of consequences for wrongful behavior. They speak of destruction, and of God's lashing out at the people God loves. But the prophets know that God demands loyalty and faithfulness. God is angry enough to destroy what has been created.

Whatever it is that makes them God's people will slowly be eaten away. Or whatever is evil within them will slowly be eaten away...like the moth slowly eats away at the cloth, like the maggots eat away at the food, like the rottenness eats away at the bones. All will be eaten away because the people have neglected to care for themselves, to do the things that ultimately lead to life. They will slowly unravel and be consumed. And then, God says, they will acknowledge their guilt, they will seek God out and, in their distress, beg for God's favor (5:15).

Isaiah tells us that those who have God's teaching in their hearts should not be afraid of the reproach of others. "For the moth will eat them [those who reproach] up like a garment, / and the worm will eat them like wool; / but my deliverance will be forever, and my salvation to all generations" (51:8). In Hosea, the Israelites have become like those who stood outside and ridiculed the name of God. Now, they too, will wear out like a moth-eaten garment.

Midwife

Yet it was you who took me from the womb, / you kept me safe on my mother's breast. / On you I was cast from my birth, / and since my mother bore me you have been my God. Psalm 22:9–10

The worshiper is clearly in distress, and the cry is haunting and familiar. We hear it again on the lips of Jesus as he is dying on the cross. "My God, my God, why have you forsaken me?" With those words Psalm 22 is ushered in. The worshiper continues, "Why are you so far from helping me, from the words of my groaning? / O my God, I cry by day, but you do not answer; / and by night, but find no rest" (vv. 1–2). The praying one knows that his ancestors cried out to God. God heard them. God saved them. And now he finds himself scorned by others, despised, and mocked. Those around him urge him to cry out to God. They think that God will not answer him (vv. 6–8).

But trust run deep in the body and soul of the one crying out to God. He has a story to tell, a testimony that bears witness to the lifelong journey and relationship he has had with the one he calls God. God was the one who brought him into the world, took him from the womb, kept him safe. God was the midwife to his miraculous birthing.

Therefore, he trusts that he can call out to this one who brought him into the world. "Do not be far from me, / for trouble is near / and there is no one to help" (v. 11). He is at the end. This is his final hope. He is at the place in his life when all he has is God.

With the enemy encircling him, his bones visible in his gaunt body, his heart melting from fear, and his body close to death, he calls out to God: "...do not be far away!" (v. 19). He turns to the divine midwife for deliverance. And when he is delivered, he does not forget the one who brought redemption. He cries out in thanksgiving and praise. And he proclaims that posterity will serve God; future generations will be told about the wonderful deliverance that God has brought. Deliverance will be proclaimed even to those whom God has not yet birthed.

This understanding of God receiving the infant as it is being born from its mother's womb is found also in Isaiah:

> Listen to me, O house of Jacob, / all the remnant of the house of Israel, / who have been borne by me from your birth, / carried from the womb; / even to your old age I am he, / even when you turn gray I will carry you. / I have made, and I will bear; / I will carry and I will save. (Isa. 46:3–4)

God has received the child and cares for it not only in its earliest years. God's care and concern has followed Israel and Jacob throughout all of its years, its entire life span.

Mother/Woman Giving Birth

You were unmindful of the Rock that bore you; / you forgot the God who gave you birth. Deuteronomy 32:18

For a long time I have held my peace, / I have kept still and restrained myself; / now I will cry out like a woman in labor, / I will gasp and pant. Isaiah 42:14

Can a woman forget her nursing child, / or show no compassion for the child of her womb? / Even these may forget, / yet I will not forget you. Isaiah 49:14–15

As a mother comforts her child, / so I will comfort you; / you shall be comforted in Jerusalem. Isaiah 66:13

The description of the pain of giving birth creates quite an image. The writer of Isaiah 42 uses an agonizing portrait to describe the expression of frustration that comes from a God whose people have left to worship carved images and who say to other images, "You are our gods." This is a God like a soldier, like a warrior, and also like a woman in labor who gasps and pants (Isa. 42:14).

This image of a God who cries out in this pain is consistent with other pictures in the Hebrew Bible of the God who is as a mother. The picture painted of the Mother God is one of a loving parent who is intimately related to the child. Speaking to Israel, the prophet speaks of a God who gives birth to a people, carries them in her womb, stays with them even until old age, and throughout all of life carries them in the journey. "I have made, and I will bear; I will carry and will save" (Isa. 46:4).

Mother God is a god of compassion and comfort. Doesn't a mother show compassion to a child? It may be possible, God admits, for a woman to forget her nursing child, but God's love is stronger than that of even the finest of mothers: "I will not forget you" (Isa.

49:15); "As a mother comforts her child, / so I will comfort you" (Isa. 66:13). It is Isaiah who brings us the many dimensions expressed in God's "mother love"—comfort, compassion, and a love that will never be forgotten.[19]

A story in Numbers 11 illustrates some of Moses' frustration with *God's children,* the Israelites, as they were traveling through the wilderness. The people were complaining about the difficult journey. They were hungry. They longed for the "good old days." They wanted meat to eat; they recalled the fish they had eaten in Egypt, and also the cucumbers, melons, leeks, onions, and the garlic. Now, they only had manna that God provided; it fell on the ground and the people gathered it and ground it and made it into cakes. But they remembered and longed for the meals they had had before the wilderness adventure began.

Moses overheard the people weeping and complaining. He was disturbed and he said to the LORD, "Why have you treated your servant so badly? Why have I not found favor in your sight, that you lay the burden of all this people on me? Did I conceive all this people? Did I give birth to them, that you should say to me, 'carry them in your bosom as a nurse carries a sucking child,' to the land that promised on oath to their ancestors?" (Num. 15:11–12). Moses is basically saying to God: "Take care of these people! You conceived them! You gave them birth! Nurse them! Take care of them!" Moses is saying: "Mother, take care of your children." Moses could not care for the people alone. The burdens were too heavy.

My Chosen Portion/My Cup

The LORD is my chosen portion and my cup; / you hold my lot. / The boundary lines have fallen for me in pleasant places; / I have a goodly heritage. Psalm 16:5

The worshiper praying to God in Psalm 16 leaves no doubt in our minds where his lot is cast, where he is willing to invest, where he wages his bets. His faith is in God. The psalmist cries out to God for protection and safety. He says to Yahweh, "You are my Lord; / I have no good apart from you" (v. 2). The psalmist speaks boldly. His words are clear and certain. He shows no ambiguity, no hesitancy. God is God. More importantly—God is *his* God. "You are *my* Lord" (emphasis added), he says. He looks to God for what he needs.

This certainty of relationship is shown again in verse 5: "The LORD is my chosen portion and my cup..." This is where the worshiper chooses to get his nourishment—his food and his drink comes from *this* portion and cup, the One who instructs and guides, and shows the worshiper the paths of living.

There is an important contrast in the psalm. The psalmist knows good and knows security because he has *chosen* God. This is not true for those who have not chosen to invest or cast their lot with this God: "Those who choose another god multiply their sorrows..." (v. 4). The worshiper knows that he has made the better choice; he has chosen the God who keeps him grounded (v. 8), brings joy (v. 9), and gives life (v. 11). To know this kind of God makes the heart glad, the soul rejoice, and the body secure (v. 9)

This choice affects all parts of our existence, whether we put our trust and reliance in God or in places and things that do not satisfy.

Parent

When Israel was a child, I loved him... Hosea 11:1

Hosea 11:1–9 is every bit as grace filled as the parable of the "prodigal son" in the New Testament. It is a story about a parent and the unending love the parent has for a child. "When Israel was a child..." It is as if God is a mother going through the well-worn photograph album and remembering all the precious moments in her children's lives: *When Israel was a child...* "I remember that I taught my child to walk. I remember when I picked up my child in my arms. I remember holding and healing my children. I led them as they went through life. I lifted them to my cheeks. I bent down to them so that I could feed them.

"But they went away. I kept calling out to them, but the more I called, the further they went away from me." We would expect the parent to turn away. We would expect the parent's anger to win the day. We would expect relationships to be severed and for the intimate bond between parent and child to be broken.

But God says… "How can I give you up?" "I will *not* execute my fierce anger; / I will not…destroy [them]; for I am God and no mortal" (Hos. 11:8–9). The final word will not be and cannot be anger. God will call them home.

It is not unusual for the prophets to use the parent/child metaphor to depict the relationship between God and people. In Isaiah, the prophetic book opens with the prophet's name and information about the historical period in which he saw his vision concerning Judah and Jerusalem. Immediately, then, the prophet calls the heavens and earth to listen and then the announcement is made by the LORD: "I reared children and brought them up, / but they have rebelled against me" (1:2a). This prelude to the rest of Isaiah names the problem: the people, God's children, no longer know God. The prophet laments that though the ox and the donkey know to whom they belong, not so with the children of God. They no longer know God who is their parent.

In Jeremiah, God through the prophet calls the faithless children to return (3:14). The children are weeping because they have perverted their way and forgotten God. God calls out to them to return; their faithlessness will be healed (3:22). In 31:18ff God struggles with the relationship God has with child Ephraim. Ephraim was like a wild animal and turned away. Now he is ashamed; he has been disgraced. God looks upon Ephraim and asks, "Is [this] the child I delight in? / As often as I speak against him, / I still remember him." The final word is that God will remember his son. "Therefore I am deeply moved for him; / I will surely have mercy on him" (v. 20).

It is interesting that the parent/child metaphor is used in the prophets to depict the heartbroken parent whose child or children have wandered away, forgotten all that the parent has done for them, wasted their inheritance, and have brought shame and disgrace upon themselves. The parent metaphor paints a vulnerable but compassionate portrait of the One who longs for the child to return home.

Potter

Woe to you who strive with your Maker, / earthen vessels with
the potter! / Does the clay say to the one who fashions it, "What
are you making"? / or "Your work has no handles"? / Woe to
anyone who says to a father, "What are you begetting?" / or to a
woman, "With what are you in labor?" Isaiah 45:9–10

In Genesis's second creation story, beginning in 2:4, God has made the earth and the heavens. There was, as yet, no plants on the earth. There were two reasons for this. First, God had not made the rain to come upon the earth to give the plants their vital nutrients. And, there was not yet someone on the earth who could till the soil and tend the plants God intended to create. The first problem was solved when a stream of water arose from the earth so that the whole face of the earth was given access to the waters of living. The second problem still lingered. So God reached down into the clay mud and formed and fashioned *adam* from the dust of the ground. In this creation story we get our first snapshot of God as potter. God makes the earth creature out of the dust of the earth. God then breathes into him the breath, or spirit, of life. God then plants a garden in Eden in the east and puts *adam* there to guard it. From the beginning, then, the storyteller wants us to know that God has created humanity out of the "stuff" of the earth and that the life of humanity is given as gift from God. We are dependent upon God for it.

This understanding of God as potter takes different forms in the hands of various biblical writers. Yahweh called out to Jeremiah and told him to go to the potter's house. (See Jer. 18.) There, God said, he would speak to Jeremiah. So Jeremiah, being Jeremiah, went. He watched the potter working at the wheel with his clay. The potter was making a vessel, and when it became spoiled, when it did not take on the form the potter intended, the potter reformed and refashioned it until it was right; until it was good.

Then Yahweh spoke to Jeremiah and said that what the potter did to the clay, God could do to the people. God could pluck up. Break down. Destroy. God could build. The image of the potter is an image of a God that is "in charge." The metaphor stresses the power of the maker over what is made. This is not like the husband/wife, parent/child, and shepherd/sheep metaphors, in which God and the people are in some kind of relationship with each other. This is not personal; the clay bears no responsibility for what happens! The clay and what it will become is in the potter's hands.

Isaiah points out the absurdity of thinking any other way. Would the earthen vessel say to the potter: "What are you making?" or, "Your work has no handles"? Of course not! That is why we sing, "Have thine own way, Lord! Have thine own way! / Thou art the potter; I am the clay."[20] The one who sings believes this is a song of trust and that God's creative power goes beyond anything we can imagine. For some, of course, this might be an image of comfort and hope. But, for others, this picture of the potter denies the co-creative power we have been given to create "new things" and to accept responsibility for our futures.

Prosecutor

Hear what the LORD says: / Rise, plead your case before the mountains, / and let the hills hear your voice. / Hear, you mountains, the controversy of the LORD... Micah 6:1–2a

The scene is the courthouse: somber, quiet. The witnesses are assembled, and perhaps the jury, too. The case is prepared, and, as always is the case in the courtroom, we are there because something has gone awry. Something is not right. There is a complaint to be made.

In Micah 6, the prosecutor is God. It is God who is bringing a lawsuit against God's people. All the mountains and all the earth are called to hear; the implications and the effects of the people's action affect the whole universe. The speech made by the prosecuting attorney is soulful and tinged with sadness and anger. "My people, what have I done to you? In what have I wearied you? Answer me!" (Mic. 6:3). God then recounts the history they have shared with each other. He reminds them that he brought them up from Egypt, redeemed them from slavery, sent Moses and Miriam and Aaron to lead them from Egypt and through the wilderness. He had saved them.

The prosecutor's accusations bring a sharp and immediate response from one who is there in the courtroom being charged with forgetting all that God has done, being charged with turning away from the steadfast God, being charged with unfaithfulness.

"What can I do," the worshiper asks, "to show you that I have not abandoned you? Shall I put together elaborate and lavish worship? Shall I bring offerings greater than anyone has ever brought before? Shall I sacrifice my firstborn child?" (6:6–7, paraphrase). The worshiper wants a reply! What does God expect? What does God want? How can life be lived so that it is God-filled and God-followed?

Someone answers: "You already know what God really requires from you... Do justice. Love kindness. Walk humbly with God" (v. 8, paraphrase). Sadly the people know that this is their covenant responsibility, and they have not lived up to it.

God rests the case.

Protector of Widows

Sing to God, sing praises to his name; / lift up a song to him who rides upon the clouds— / his name is the L<small>ORD</small>— / be exultant before him. / Father of orphans and protector of widows / is God in his holy habitation. / God gives the desolate a home to live in; / he leads out the prisoners to prosperity, / but the rebellious live in a parched land. Psalm 68:4–6

The Old Testament paints graphic portraits of the plights of widows. Naomi had moved with her husband Elimelech to the land of Moab, where there was food and where they could raise their family. Naomi's husband died, as did her sons (Ruth 1). She was left with two daughters-in-law; one of them, Ruth, accompanied her back to her native land, to Bethlehem, to care for her. Naomi had no one to protect her; she had no way to feed herself; she had no one to give her status in the community. It was through Ruth and Boaz, her kinsman and redeemer that she found a way to survive and even thrive in a land where she was the least of the least, one of the vulnerable.

Or remember the widow of Zarephath (1 Kings 17:8–16). God sent Elijah to find her, and, when he got to the city gates, she was there. She was gathering sticks, hoping to scrape together enough firewood to cook the meal she had stored in her kitchen—only enough meal for one cake, and then she and her son would probably die.

These two narratives show the desperate plight of the widow in Old Testament society. In addition, the laws in Exodus and Deuteronomy also demonstrate how vulnerable they were. There are frequent reminders to the people that they must consider the needs of the stranger, the widow, and the orphan. These must have deserved and needed special attention and care. (See Ex. 22:22; Deut. 10:18; 14:29; 16:11, 14; 24:19, 20, 21; 26: 12, 13; 17:19.) In Exodus, we get a glimpse of how important it was to God that these be treated fairly and with respect: You shall not wrong or oppress a resident alien [stranger], for you were aliens [strangers] in the land of Egypt. You shall not abuse any widow or orphan. If you do abuse them, when they cry out to me, I will surely heed their cry; my wrath will burn, and I will kill you with the sword, and your wives shall become widows and your children orphans (22:21–24).

The consequences for mistreating the widow, orphan, or stranger were great! This was important business.

In Deuteronomy, the writer is reminding the people of the essence of the law, the great principles upon which it was built. The people are reminded that Yahweh was their God and is the "God of gods and Lord of lords, the great God, mighty and awesome" (Deut. 10:17). How do we know the greatness of this God? This God "executes justice for the orphan and the widow, and…loves the strangers, providing them food and clothing" (v. 18). Thus, in the laws that follow, the people are commanded to treat others as God would treat them.

In the Psalms God is called the protector of the widow. In the prophets we are called not to oppress (rather, to *care for*) the most vulnerable around us. (See Isaiah 9:17; Jeremiah 7:6; Zechariah 7:10; Malachi 3:5.) We are led to believe that this may be our most important task!

Redeemer

Answer me, O Lord, for your steadfast love is good; / according to your abundant mercy, turn to me. / Do not hide your face from your servant, / for I am in distress—make haste to answer me. / Draw near to me, redeem me. Psalm 69:16–18a

Generations have been intrigued by the story of Naomi and her two daughters-in-law, Orpah and Ruth. (See Ruth 1—4.) Faced with the devastating realities of loss and famine, they begin to forge their way into the world, taking risks and pledging support for and solidarity with one another. At the crossroads, Ruth, a Moabite, makes the decision not to return to her homeland but to travel to Bethlehem with her mother-in-law, now without husband, son, or grandchild. The pleasant one, Naomi, has become bitter, empty. She thought Yahweh had brought calamity upon her, but she was to find that God had not forsaken her.

This is a story about redemption. In Israelite society, a man's nearest relative (brother, uncle, cousin, or another kinsman) was responsible for standing up for him and maintaining his rights. There was a strong sense of tribal solidarity. Members of the clan and their possessions held a certain kind of unity. Disruptions in the unity were not tolerable and had to be restored. In this story, Boaz is the redeemer or *go'el*. There is a closer relative to Elimelech, Naomi's deceased husband, but he is not willing to buy the property for Naomi because he would also be required to marry her daughter-in-law to "maintain the dead man's name on his inheritance" (4:5). Boaz, next in line, is willing. He buys the field for the family and marries Ruth, and together they provide Naomi with a grandson and, consequently, renewed standing in the community.

The redeemer had other responsibilities. If an Israelite sold himself to a foreigner as a slave, the redeemer could buy him back or redeem him. If someone was murdered, the redeemer, who would kill the murderer or a member of the killer's clan, could avenge the death. A redeemer could also be the one who would appear as a "helper" in a lawsuit to see that justice was done. A redeemer cared about the family member's rights and honor.

Yahweh performs a similar role when Yahweh is described as the "redeemer" of the fatherless and widowed by pleading their cause (Prov. 23:11). Yahweh takes up the cause of the worshiper and redeems his life (Lam. 3:58). In the Old Testament God redeems people from:

    evil
    violence
    oppression
    the hand of the enemy
    distress
    dangers in travel
    imprisonment
    illness
    death
    sin

In Exodus, God promises to bring the people out from under the burden of the Egyptians, to redeem them with outstretched arm. God redeemed the people from slavery. Redemption, then, has something to do with being delivered, being drawn out from one world into another, being saved from that which oppresses, confines, frightens, or destroys.

Yahweh is the redeemer. God is capable of drawing us out from one world into another, from the world of sin into one of forgiveness, from fear to courage, from oppression to a resistant voice that challenges that oppression.

There are many calls in the Psalms from worshipers who desire that God redeem them. And there is the assurance that God will. Often the question is…*when?* When will this deliverance take place? Must redemption come in its own time?[21]

Refuge

Lead me to the rock / that is higher than I; / for you are my refuge, / a strong tower against the enemy. Psalm 61:2b–3

You would confound the plans of the poor, / but the LORD is their refuge. Psalm 14:6

Protect me, O God, for in you I take refuge. Psalm 16:1

In you, O Lord, I seek refuge; / do not let me ever be put to shame; / in your righteousness deliver me. / Incline your ear to me; / rescue me speedily. / Be a rock of refuge for me, / a strong fortress to save me. Psalm 31:1–2

It often comes as a cry of affirmation in God's trustworthy presence. The psalmists cry out in their despair, their disease, and their loneliness. They make a public proclamation that they put their trust in God. "You are my refuge." "In you I take refuge." "Be a...refuge for me."

Often that refuge is described as a place that is high and lifted up. The refuge is a place that lifts the one who is praying up above the fray, the noise, and the scoffing and humiliation that one has to endure. It is like the high mountains for the wild goats (Ps. 104:18), or like the highest defense tower that elevates the one in danger and takes him out of harm's way. The psalmist tries to imagine a place where he is safe. He just wants to be safe.

It is "in God" that safety is found. The word translated "refuge" expresses an understanding that is central to the Psalter. The term confirms and instructs believers to live a life that is totally dependent, "refuged" in God.[22] Those involved in dangerous tasks often use Psalm 91. It has been carried to the battlefield by soldiers who feel a heightened need for protection. In the psalm there are multiple words and phrases relating to the need of God's protection and care: "shelter," "shadow of the Almighty," "refuge, "fortress," "trust," "he will deliver," "cover," "shield," "buckler," "dwelling place," "no evil shall befall you," "guard." This psalm speaks of God's unfailing presence during times of test and trouble. God is seen as the rescuer, the one who will deliver and save.

Rock

For who is God except the Lord? / And who is a rock besides our God? Psalm 18:31

Let the words of my mouth and the meditation of my heart / be

acceptable to you, / O LORD, *my rock and my redeemer.*
Psalm 19:14

*The Rock, his work is perfect / and all his ways are just. / A
faithful God, without deceit, / just and upright is he; / yet his
degenerate children have dealt falsely with him, / a perverse and
crooked generation.* Deuteronomy 32:4

There are three Hebrew words that translate as "rock," and
together they are used about one hundred times in the Old Testament.
Two of the three are used as metaphorical names for God.[23] This
metaphor is multidimensional and draws forth varied meanings
and emotions.

Boulder, rock, strength, endurance—God was these things to the
psalmists. In their times of trouble and adversity, God was always
there. To understand God as rock was, on the one hand, to see God as
enduring, everlasting, and sure. Like the strongest rock that seems to
withstand the elements and that never changes, God was dependable
and certain. This marked the difference, in the prophets' minds,
between God and humanity. Unlike the mighty Rock, the people
in covenant with God were often fickle and couldn't be depended
upon for loyalty and faithfulness.

To understand God as rock was also to understand God as the
sure foundation, something more solid and firm than shifting sand.
God was a secure and certain place to stand. To see God as rock is to
see more than certainty or foundation. It is to see God as powerful,
as one who not only wanted to save and deliver, but also could. The
God who is as a rock could defend against the strongest enemy.

The connection to rock, however, was something even more.
The craggy rocks on the mountainside were scarred with crevices,
clefts. There, the psalmists thought, were places they could hide.
God as rock sometimes meant God as refuge. In these places, safe
and secure, the worshiper could escape from the tribulations of life,
the chaos that surrounded him, the never-ending challenges that
life was bringing.

How interesting it is, then, that it is in a rock that Moses finds
his "escape" not from the world, but from God! Moses asked to see
God's glory, and Yahweh answers, "I will make all my goodness pass

before you, and will proclaim before you the name, 'The Lord'" (Ex. 33:19). But God then said no one is able to see the face of God and live. So, while the glory of God passed by, God put Moses in a cleft of the rock. God covered Moses with his hand until he had passed by. When he took away his hand, Moses saw God's back, but his face he did not see.

The cleft in the rock is also the place where the prophets said people were hiding from God:

> The terror you inspire / and the pride of your heart have deceived you, / you who live in the clefts of the rock, / who hold the height of the hill. / Although you make your nest as high as the eagle's, / from there I will bring you down. (Jer. 49:16; see also Ob. 1:3)

Those who live high in the clefts, who soar like eagles, and whose nests are set among the stars God will find and bring down the proud.

Salvation

> *I will give thanks to you, O Lord, / for though you were angry with me, / your anger turned away, / and you comforted me. / Surely God is my salvation; / I will trust, and will not be afraid, / for the Lord God is my strength and my might; / he has become my salvation.* Isaiah 12:1–2

The Israelites under the leadership of Moses had left Egypt and were beginning their journey toward a land they had never seen, never known. As they began the long and torturous journey, they set up camp between Migdol and the sea, just as Yahweh had told them. When Pharaoh found out that the Israelites had left, he regretted having let them go. He took the chariots and the officers over them, and they began to pursue the Israelites, who had made a temporary home by the sea. The Israelites looked back and saw the Egyptians advancing on them. They were afraid, and they cried out to the Lord and to Moses:

> "It would have been better for us to serve the Egyptians than to die in the wilderness." But Moses said to the people, "Do

not be afraid, stand firm, and see the deliverance [salvation] that the LORD will accomplish for you today; for the Egyptians whom you see today you shall never see again. The LORD will fight for you, and you have only to keep still." (Ex. 14:12b–14)

The rest of the story is one of the most well-known Old Testament narratives. Popularized by film and painting, we hold in our mind images of Moses stretching out his hand over the sea, and the waves dividing to let the Israelites pass on to freedom. At the end of the story, the narrator says to us, "Thus the LORD saved Israel that day" (v. 30a).

Exodus 15 preserves the words of a very old hymn. Moses and the Israelites, having crossed the sea, sing this song to Yahweh: "The LORD is my strength and my might, / and he has become my salvation" (v. 2a).

Experts think that the word translated "salvation" may be related to the word meaning "spacious and wide." God can deliver us from what restricts and oppresses us. We are given room, a liberating space, within which we can live our lives. God brought the Israelites from Egypt, from the small confined space by the edge of the sea, through the narrow path in the middle of the sea, out into freedom on the other side.

Salvation in the Old Testament is something that can happen time and again. Over and over, God delivers. "God is my salvation" means that God actively participates in the life of the community. God hears our cries of distress and God is willing and desirous that we be given full and wide berth to live out life abundantly. God delivers us from restricted, oppressive places. That is why the psalmist could say that God drew him out of the raging waters that threatened to carry him away. God delivered him from the enemy and from those who were too strong for him. God supported him and brought him out "into a broad place"[24] (Ps. 18:19) where life could be lived fully and freely.

The psalmists cry out and urgently ask God to save them. They also make strong affirmations of faith that God is the author of their salvation. Of the 150 Psalms, over one third of them mention salvation or being saved by God!

The cries for salvation come for individuals; they also come from the community and for the nation. *Save me! Save us! Save!* Sometimes this is translated *Help me!* or *Deliver me!* These are urgent appeals from the worshiper wanting to be saved from the persecution of many enemies, from grief and the shedding of tears, or from any of a number of difficulties: loneliness, feelings of forsakenness, shame, deep and rising flood waters, the wicked, or simply the state of being poor and needy. The psalmists want to be saved "in love."

Often at the conclusion of a psalm there is an affirmation that God can and will save. The psalmist lives with the assurance that whatever life is bringing him, God can and will deliver him from disaster.

Shade/Shadow

For you have been a refuge to the poor, / a refuge to the needy in their distress, / a shelter from the rainstorm and a shade from the heat. / When the blast of the ruthless was like a winter rainstorm, / the noise of aliens like heat in a dry place, / you subdued the heat with the shade of clouds; / the song of the ruthless was stilled. Isaiah 25:4–5

Guard me as the apple of the eye; / hide me in the shadow of your wings. Psalm 17:8

You who live in the shelter of the Most High, / who abide in the shadow of the Almighty, / will say to the Lord, *"My refuge and my fortress; / my God in whom I trust." / For he will deliver you from the snare of the fowler / and from the deadly pestilence; / he will cover you with his pinions, / and under his wings you will find refuge; / his faithfulness is a shield and a buckler.*
Psalm 91:1–4

It is relief from intense heat on a very warm day, given by even the smallest of branches that cast a shadow to guard us from the raging sun. There we rest and stop our movement. Our skin is protected, even if just for a moment, from relentless rays.

It is the relief we feel when we can find a place to rest, safe and secure, from our enemies. Our fear diminishes, our pulse slows down. No one can find us.

God is this relief, this place, where one can rest from the rainstorm and recover from the heat. Under the wings of the mother eagle we rest because she will protect and watch out for us.

This image of God is not unlike that of the shield and the buckler. God protects. But it suggests something more intimate and relational. God is like the mother eagle that protects with her wings, because we belong to her. She has given us birth. She is the place where we return over and over and over again, because she will always be there for us.

Isaiah uses the metaphors of shade and shelter as a prelude to a beautiful hymn about the end times, when there will be on the mountain a great feast for all people. The prophet envisions a time when death will be swallowed up and tears will be wiped from all eyes (Isa. 25:6–10a).

The prophet gives praise to the God who has done wonderful things. In particular the prophet praises the God who brings relief from oppression:

> For you have been a refuge to the poor, / a refuge to the needy in their distress, / a shelter from the rainstorm and a shade from the heat. / When the blast of the ruthless was like a winter rainstorm, / the noise of aliens like heat in a dry place, / you subdued the heat with the shade of clouds; / the song of the ruthless was stilled. (Isa. 25:4–5)

God is the shelter for those who are oppressed, pushed down and abused by the world. The prophet sees the day when oppressions will be lifted and removed, and these will know freedom.

Shepherd

The LORD is my shepherd, I shall not want. Psalm 23:1

He will feed his flock like a shepherd; / he will gather the lambs in his arms, / and carry them in his bosom, / and gently lead the mother sheep. Isaiah 40:11

It is, perhaps, one of the most recognized and best-loved verses of Hebrew scripture: "The LORD is my shepherd…" The rendering of this first verse of the Twenty-third Psalm brings memories of people and places and times past: a funeral of a loved one, perhaps; or a baptism; memories of learning those first verses of scripture as a child.

The Psalms bears witness to God as a shepherd: one who cares for the flock, who cares for each individual sheep in the flock. "The LORD is my shepherd, I shall not want." This is the shepherd who provides everything the flock needs—green pastures for food and nourishment, still waters for drink. The sheep lack nothing. The shepherd brings restoration. Even when the sheep walk through the darkest and most frightening valley, the shepherd is there for protection. The shepherd never leaves or abandons; he guides. There is an intimate relationship between shepherd and animal.

It is important for us not only to understand God as shepherd, but to ask a very important question: *What kind of shepherd?* Both Jeremiah and Ezekiel, in describing leaders of the people who are charged with the task of "shepherding," acknowledge that not all shepherds go about their work in ways that are healthy and life-producing for their flocks. There are shepherds who destroy and scatter the sheep. They drive the sheep away and do not attend to them (Jer. 23:4). The sheep are afraid and dismayed. Some are missing. This is not the kind of shepherd God is. God gathers the flock to feed, guide, and protect them. This is the portrait painted of a great, gathering God. In Second Isaiah, the prophet speaks to the community in exile, making proclamation and promise about a God who looks upon the community that is scattered and torn away from its homeland. God is the shepherd who will gather all of them up in his arms and guide them back safely home.

While the metaphor of shepherd is not used often in the Old Testament, the beloved Twenty-third Psalm has made it a favorite one. The best description of God as the "Good Shepherd" comes from the prophet Ezekiel:

> I myself will search for my sheep, and will seek them out. As shepherds seek out their flocks when they are among their scattered sheep, so I will seek out my sheep. I will rescue them from all the places to which they have been scattered on a day of clouds and thick darkness. I will bring them out from the peoples and gather them from the countries, and will bring them into their own land; and I will feed them

on the mountains of Israel, by the watercourses, and in all
the inhabited parts of the land. I will feed them with good
pasture, and the mountain heights of Israel shall be their
pasture; there they shall lie down in good grazing land, and
they shall feed on rich pasture on the mountains of Israel.
I myself will be the shepherd of my sheep, and I will make
them lie down, says the Lord GOD. I will seek the lost, and I
will bring back the strayed, and I will bind up the injured,
and I will strengthen the weak, but the fat and the strong I
will destroy. I will feed them with justice. (Ezek. 34:11–16)

Are the last lines a surprise to you? What do they mean? How
are they consistent with an understanding of a God who favors the
poor and the disinherited?

Shower

*Come let us return to the LORD; / for it is he who has torn, and he
will heal us; / he has struck down, and he will bind us up. / After
two days he will revive us; / on the third day he will raise us up,
/ that we may live before him. / Let us know, let us press on to
know the LORD; / his appearing is as sure as the dawn; / he will
come to us like the showers, / like the spring rains that water the
earth.* Hosea 6:1–3

The prophet Hosea clearly names the demise of the people. They
have been unfaithful to their God. Through the compelling story of
Hosea and Gomer in chapters 1—3, the disloyalty of the people is
graphically depicted, as is the grief and anger of the God who longs
to be in relationship with them. These words of accusation and
indictment are woven through the book of Hosea. But these are not
the only words Hosea speaks. Hosea also speaks some dramatic words
of comfort and restoration. He speaks words of hope. If the people
return to Yahweh, they will know healing. God will bind them up.
They will be revived once again for their living.

God will come to them, Hosea says, because his appearing is
as sure as the dawn. "He will come to us like the showers, / like
the spring rains that water the earth." Why does Hosea use these

words to describe the way that God makes Godself known? Is God's coming to us like the rain because the rain renews the earth and makes growth possible? Is God's coming like the rain because water is needed for life? or because showers come to all parts of the earth? Is it because it is rainwater that changes desert and wilderness into meadow and forest?

The prophet Isaiah gives us some clues about what this image might mean:

> For as the rain and snow come down from heaven, / and do not return there until they have watered the earth, / making it bring forth and sprout, / giving seed to the sower and bread to the eater, / so shall my word be that goes out from mouth; / it shall not return to me empty, / but it shall accomplish that which I purpose, / and succeed in the thing for which I sent it. (Isa. 55:10–11)

God's coming to us, God's word, is like the rain because it makes possible a seed's growth. And, ultimately, then, it brings forth bread and nourishment for the community. Rainwater has a purpose. It fulfills its purpose, as does the word of God that comes forth to us.

Song

Then Moses and the Israelites sang this song to the Lord: "I will sing to the Lord, for he has triumphed gloriously; / horse and rider he has thrown into the sea. / The Lord is my strength and my [song], / and he has become my salvation; / this is my God, and I will praise him, / my father's God, and I will exalt him.
Exodus 15:1–2

All nations surrounded me; / in the name of the Lord I cut them off! / They surrounded me, surrounded me on every side; / in the name of the Lord I cut them off! / They surrounded me like bees; / they blazed like a fire of thorns; / in the name of the Lord I cut them off! / I was pushed hard, so that I was falling, / but the

LORD *helped me. / The* LORD *is my strength and my [song]; / he has become my salvation.* Psalm 118:10–14

The Psalms are about singing. Many of the Psalms are laments, and they depict in graphic detail the plights of the worshipers who are surrounded by the enemy, who are sick, who are outcast. But almost without exception these Psalms end in outbursts of praise and singing. The one who is in despair knows that God will come to save or heal. There are also Psalms of thanksgiving. These express joy and gratitude for all that God is and does in the world. In all of these, there are calls to sing out. The Psalms are about singing.

But for those who have known danger and have been delivered from it, God not only deserves our response in song, God *is* the song. "Yahweh is my strength and my song..."

In 1858, Anna Julia Cooper was born in Raleigh, North Carolina, to her mother, a slave, and her father, her mother's master. Anna became one of the most highly educated and intellectual black women of her century. Teacher, administrator, and scholar, Cooper received her Ph.D. at the Sorbonne. Her dissertation was entitled "Attitudes toward Slavery in Revolutionary France."

Like other prestigious black women of her time, she sought to implement a vision of freedom and justice. It was through her *A Voice from the South,* published in 1892, that Cooper questioned and challenged the domination of the weak by the strong in our culture. She attacked the evils of racism and sexism and classicism.

Dr. Cooper was also quite a theologian. In one of her writings she explored different metaphors for God. She described God's presence as a divine spark, a shadow, a cell. Most interesting, however, is her designation of God as the "Singing Something." This "Singing Something" is what moved her toward speaking for freedom and equality. God's voice sings within us, she said. All human voices must be added to the chorus, she thought, because we are not created in the image, but in the sound, of God.

It was the singing something within her that gave her the courage to speak up and speak out. It was the singing something that moved her out of safe silence. God was her song.[25]

Stronghold of the Oppressed

The Lord is a stronghold for the oppressed, / a stronghold in times of trouble. Psalm 9:9

When Israel was in Egypt's land; let my people go,
oppressed so hard they could not stand, let my people go...
The Lord told Moses what to do, let my people go,
to lead the Hebrew children through, let my people go.
—"Go Down, Moses" (Negro spiritual)[26]

"Go Down, Moses" is just one of the many, many spirituals that attest to a God who is ultimately and intimately interested in the plight of the oppressed. It is God who hears their cries; it is God who will deliver.

We shall overcome, we shall overcome, we shall overcome
   someday!
Oh, deep in my heart I do believe we shall overcome
   someday!
The Lord will see us through, the Lord will see us through, the
   Lord will see us through someday.
Oh, deep in my heart I do believe the Lord will see us through
   someday.   —"We Shall Overcome"[27]

That is the fundamental belief of the psalmist. God is his stronghold. He has known oppression from the enemy. He has known the mercy of God and now his enemies have vanished; even their memory has perished. God has brought justice, and justice means that the most vulnerable, those who are oppressed by the world and its powers, have been liberated. They have been freed. They have overcome.

God is the stronghold of these. God is the one they depend on. God sustains them. They hold onto the God who is faithful to them. It is, perhaps, all that they have, the only place they can turn. It is the place where they can find strength in the midst of despair, pain, suffering, and humiliation.

Suffering One

I reared children and brought them up, / but they have rebelled against me. / The ox knows its owner, / and the donkey its master's crib; / but Israel does not know, / my people do not understand. Isaiah 1:2–3

The prophets in the Old Testament name clearly the realities and conditions of the people who are in a covenant relationship with God. While the books of the prophets contain many words of grace, restoration, and hope, they also contain clear indictments and honest renderings of the ways the people have been unfaithful and have turned away. Many of those prophets describe a God who is suffering because the people have turned away. God asks, Why? Why have you strayed from me? Why have you left me and turned away? God laments.

In the Genesis flood story, God looked upon the wickedness of the people, and God was sorry that God had created humanity. God was sorry, and it grieved God's heart. Psalm 78:40–41 says: "How often they rebelled against him in the wilderness / and grieved him in the desert! / They tested God again and again, / and provoked the Holy One of Israel." God was grieving, and a repeated theme in the Old Testament is that God will seek every conceivable means to keep the relationship intact. Throughout history God shows a salvific will, a deep and abiding desire, to be in relationship with the people.

These stories attest to a kind of suffering that God experiences; it is a suffering that comes *because* of the people. There is also a different kind of suffering attested in the Old Testament. It is God suffering *with* the people.

In the beginning of the exodus story, the Israelites are slaves in the land of Egypt. They moan and cry out to God because of their sorrow, and God has heard: "I have observed the misery of my people who are in Egypt; I have heard their cry on account of their taskmasters. Indeed, I know their sufferings, and I have come down to deliver them from the Egyptians" (Ex. 3:7–8a). This is not a God who is detached from the people. This is not a distant God. This is a God who sees and hears despair and who is moved and who delivers.

The Psalms present a strong portrait of a God who is with the people in their times of trouble: "I will be with them in trouble" (Ps. 91:15). Even walking through the darkest of valleys, the worshiper says about Yahweh, "you are with me" (Ps. 23:4).

The God of the Old Testament is present with those in their difficult times, times of fear and peril. When disaster or tragedy strikes, God becomes the one who weeps and laments. God suffers with God's people.[28]

In the book of Jeremiah (2—9), the reader witnesses an abrupt change in the character of Yahweh. At first, Yahweh is the jealous and abusive God, angry at Israel (his bride and wife) for her unfaithfulness. But in the latter part of this unit, a remarkable transformation occurs as we witness the tearful, sorrowful God who is lamenting the plight of his people. God's tears portray a brokenhearted husband. Some may see this portrayal of the suffering, weeping God as too vulnerable, too weak. But the tears provide the possibility for healing. Perhaps there is a "balm in Gilead." (See Jer. 8:18—9:1.) God draws near, abandons fury, leaves aside honor. God joins in the people's suffering. God breaks from his role as dominating prideful male, the mighty warrior, and for a brief interlude participates in the pain of the people. This is a God who is fluid, changing, repenting. This is a God who is unpredictable and uncontainable. This God is deeply relational and can vacate sovereignty and transcendence to relate to the other.[29]

Sun

O LORD God of hosts, hear my prayer; / give ear, O God of Jacob!
/ Behold our shield, O God; / look on the face of your anointed.
/ For a day in your courts is better / than a thousand elsewhere.
/ I would rather be a doorkeeper in the house of my God / than
live in the tents of wickedness. / For the LORD God is a sun and
shield; / he bestows favor and honor. Psalm 84:8–11

The psalmist (Ps. 84) has found a place, a home, in God. "How lovely is your dwelling place, / O LORD of hosts!" (v. 1). Most every verse reinforces this wonderful portrait of one who can think of no more wonderful, meaningful, secure place than in the house of

God: "My soul longs… / for the courts of the Lord" (v. 2a); "my heart and flesh sing for joy / to the living God" (v. 2b). The altars are the psalmist's home. "Happy are those who live in your house" (v. 4a); "Happy are those whose strength is in you" (v. 5a). To be in the courts, the house of God is better, a thousand times over, than anywhere else. This psalm is filled with overflowing joy and unending praise.

Why? Because "the Lord God is a sun and shield" (v. 11a). What does this mean?

Often in the Hebrew Bible we're reminded that it is God who has created the sun. And often we're reminded that it is God who controls the sun; God makes the day the day and the night the night. God can turn day into night and can cause a cloud to cover the sun so it does not shine. But God as sun? Is God a sun because God sheds light? Is it because God bestows glory upon those God has created? Is God like a sun because God, like the created sun, is so powerful and affects our everyday living? Is it because God makes our everyday living possible?

Sustainer

I lie down and sleep; / I wake again, for the Lord sustains me.
Psalm 3:5

The title indicates that Psalm 3 is a psalm of David. It is a song he was to have sung when he fled from his son Absalom. It is a song of terror. David feels that his foes are many, and they surround him. He puts his trust in God, but many are saying to him, "There is no help for you in God." He is ridiculed and mocked because he believes God walks with him.

"I lie down and sleep; / I wake again, for the Lord sustains me" (v. 5). David knows that God is with him, despite the jeering from tens of thousands who have set themselves against him. It is that knowledge that makes it possible for him to simply make it through another day. *One step at a time*. He goes to bed. He wakes up to face it all one more time. And he can do this because God is there.

In Psalm 51, the psalmist asks God to create within him a clean heart. The following verses are beloved by many.

Create in me a clean heart, O God, / and put a new and right spirit within me. / Do not cast me away from your presence, / and do not take your holy spirit from me. / Restore to me the joy of your salvation, / and sustain in me a willing spirit. (vv. 10–12)

The psalmist recognizes that it is God who gifts us with generous, willing, free spirits. God not only sustains our living, but God also sustains our goodness and allows righteousness to grow within us.

The One Who Lifts Up My Head

For he will hide me in his shelter / in the day of trouble; / he will conceal me under the cover of his tent; / he will set me high on a rock. / Now my head is lifted up / above my enemies all around me, / and I will offer in his tent / sacrifices with shouts of joy; / I will sing and make melody to the Lord. Psalm 27:5–6

Downcast eyes, a face etched with lines caused by worry and despair—it is not difficult to think of the times in life that we have come upon people whose presence speaks sadness; there is no glint of hopefulness. These are ones who have known profound loss—of person or home. Perhaps they know great regret or shame. Or failure. Their enemy or oppressor beats them down. They can no longer face the world that surrounds them; it is too much for them to bear.

The psalmist knows these times; he has experienced them. He asks, "The Lord is my light and my salvation; / whom shall I fear?" (Ps. 27:1a). Though the enemy is encamped against him, he looks to God to hide him in a shelter, to conceal him in a tent, or to set him high on a rock.

It is God who will lift the psalmist's head. It is God who will raise his downcast eyes. It is God who will not forsake him. God will deliver; God will not "give him up" to the experiences in life that threaten to destroy him. The psalmist ends his singing with an affirmation of unconditional hope: "I believe that I shall see the goodness of the Lord / in the land of the living" (Ps. 27:13).

Vineyard Owner

Let me sing for my beloved / my love song concerning his vineyard... Isaiah 5:1

It's a love song about devotion and betrayal. Maybe that makes it a country love song or the blues. It is about a vineyard owner who had a plot of land; it was very fertile hill. The owner dug it and cleared it of stones. He planted choice vines, the very best, and he put a tower in the middle of the field so that it could be watched and protected.

He built a wine vat; he was certain that the land would yield a good crop. He had done everything that could be done. But alas... the field yielded sour grapes, wild grapes. No wine could be made from them. What more could he have done?

The people listening to Isaiah singing this song (Isa. 5) would have easily answered the question—"nothing!" Nothing more could be done. The landowner invested his time and his money. He had done all that a farmer could do. The landowner was angry. He broke down the walls of the vineyard and made the land a waste. The field did not fulfill its purpose. It was useless.

The people would agree, but Isaiah goes on. You, Israel, you are the vineyard. God has cultivated you and invested in you. God had expectations for you. God expected a harvest of justice and righteousness, but hears only violence and cries. The *people* had been God's beloved.

In other places, God begins to sing again. God continues to sing to the people of Israel and draws them back into relationship. He sends prophets to invite them into lives that produce justice and righteousness. But not here. Here the song ends as the people live into the consequences of their living.[30]

Voice

The voice of the Lord *is over the waters; / the God of glory thunders, / the* Lord, *over mighty waters. / The voice of the* Lord

is powerful; / the voice of the LORD is full of majesty.
Psalm 29:3–4

Sometimes we tame God. We make God understandable and
palatable, friendly and kind. Sometimes we forget that to which the
psalmists attest—that this God we worship is strong and jealous and
incensed when we fail to work toward justice and righteousness in
the world in which we live. We forget the awesome nature of the
One who is larger and greater than can be imagined.

Thus the psalmist pleads to the people to remember: "Ascribe
to the LORD glory and strength. / Ascribe to the LORD the glory of his
name..." (Ps. 29:1b–2a). The worshipers are reminded about the sheer
power of this God whom they worship. His voice...

> is over the waters,
> thunders,
> is powerful,
> is full of majesty,
> breaks the cedars,
> flashes forth flames of fire,
> shakes the wilderness,
> causes the oaks to whirl, and
> strips the forest bare.

The voice of this God is so powerful that it can alter the landscape
and make giant trees topple.

The prophet Elijah was once on the top of Mount Carmel (1 Kings
18:20–40). He was challenging the prophets of Baal to a contest.
He told the 450 prophets of Baal and the 400 prophets of Asherah
that they needed to make a decision; they were limping about on
two opinions. "If you want to worship Yahweh," he said to them,
"worship Yahweh; but if you want to worship Baal, worship Baal."
He was saying to them—make up your minds and commit yourself
to one God or the other.

Elijah said to the people, "Let two bulls be given to us; let them
choose one bull for themselves, cut it in pieces, and lay it on the
wood, but put no fire to it; I will prepare the other bull and lay it
on the wood, but put no fire to it" (v. 23). Elijah encouraged the

prophets, then, to call on the name of their gods. The bulls were prepared and the prophets of Baal called upon him from morning until noon. There was no answer. Elijah mocked them and said that perhaps their god had wandered away or was on a journey. Perhaps he was sleeping. They cried again and, as midday passed, they raved on. But...the narrator tells us that *there was no voice.* In the story, this is the difference between the real god and false gods. The false gods have no voice and cannot speak and be truly present in the community.

Then Elijah repaired the altar and put twelve stones upon it. He called for water to be poured upon the burnt offering and the wood. Three times the altar was drenched with water. Elijah called upon Yahweh, and the fire of Yahweh fell and consumed the burnt offering, the wood, the stones, and the dust, and licked up the water that was in the trench. The people recognized this as the work of the true God, saying, "The Lord indeed is God; the Lord indeed is God." (See v. 39.)[31]

The voice of God can come as great thunder. It came to the boy Samuel in the temple as the voice of a stranger calling his name. It came to Elijah on the mountainside as a sound of sheer silence. The voice of God comes as it needs to come.

Warrior

I hear, and I tremble within; / my lips quiver at the sound. / Rottenness enters into my bones, / and my steps tremble beneath me. / I wait quietly for the day of calamity / to come upon the people who attack us. Habakkuk 3:16

It is often accompanied with cosmic chaos: Yahweh as the warrior who is going out to destroy and demolish the nations that have defeated or oppressed the Israelites. In Habakkuk 3, the prophet is anticipating the time when God will overwhelm and defeat their enemies. God's glory covers the heavens. The earth was filled with praise. There was a brightness, like the sun; rays came forth from God's hand; that is where the power was hidden. There was pestilence and plagues. Yahweh stopped and shook the earth; the eternal mountains were shattered. The hills sank low. The mountains writhed and a torrent of water swept by. The moon stood still at the light of God's arrows passing by. God was coming to save God's people.

The Psalms describe this warrior God who carries a shield and marches through the wilderness before God's people. This God rides his chariot and shatters the enemy. This God breaks the enemies' teeth, and uses his sword. This God swallows up enemies and puts them to flight. He aims with the bow and shoots arrows. This God brings desolation.[32] The understanding of God as warrior is prevalent in the first two books of the Psalms, but not in the latter three. (See Psalms 3; 5; 7; 10; 17; 18; 21; 35; 38; 46; 59; 64; 68.)

In Psalm 21 the psalmist extols the God who gives victory to the king. God will make of the enemy a fiery furnace. Yahweh will swallow them in his wrath and fire will consume them. What are we to do with these images of the warrior God? What do we think about the God who leads the Israelites over the Jordan River and promises to destroy the enemy so that God's people can make their home in the land promised to them?

In this world where violence runs rampant and war drains our energy and resources at every turn, what do we "do" with the warrior? Does this give permission for "just war"? Or do we simply see this "picture" of God as one that the Israelites borrowed from the cultures around them? Is this another metaphor that has outlived its usefulness? Is it a metaphor appropriated over the centuries in ways that have brought unnecessary war, death, and destruction? Do we, like the Israelites, assume that *our* enemies are God's enemies? What shall we do? How shall we live?[33]

Wrestler

Jacob was left alone; and a man wrestled with him until daybreak. Genesis 32:24

Jacob stands by the edge of the river. He is alone. Already the stage is set in Genesis 32 for an adventure. What will happen to the man who, in his youth, deceived his aging, blind father and tricked him into giving Jacob the family's birthright? What will happen to this man who then traveled to the north and through scheming and deception amassed a large fortune? And what will happen to him now as he prepares to be reunited with his brother again? Will he lose his life? He sends family and friends ahead to prepare the way, perhaps to "soften" brother Esau so that their meeting will not be violent or fatal. We wonder, and Jacob wonders, and he sends his wives and maids and eleven children to the other side of the river, and he is alone. And it is night.

A man wrestles him. What man? Who is the man? Is this God? An angel or messenger? A thief? A stranger? It is not unlike our wrestling in the night with fears and regrets, with conscience. And when the man sees that he cannot prevail against Jacob, he strikes him on the hip socket, putting it out of joint. "Let me go," the stranger says, "for the day is breaking" (v. 26a). But Jacob replies, "I will not let you go, unless you bless me" (v. 26b). We wonder if, as Jacob prepares to face the brother who has vowed to kill him (Gen. 27:41), the blessing might have something to do with Jacob's life. He no longer can rely on his own wits and resources. He prays all night long, becoming the father of his people. What is it he fights so persistently for?

Jacob wrestles with a wrestler. Jacob believes he wrestles with God, who says, "What is your name?" (v. 27), to which Jacob replies, not surprisingly, "Jacob" (v. 27). God says, from this day on,

> "You shall no longer be called Jacob, but Israel, for you have striven [wrestled] with God and with humans, and have prevailed." Then Jacob asked him, "Please tell me your name." But he said, "Why is it that you ask my name?" (v. 29) And there he blessed him. So Jacob called the place Peniel, saying, "For I have seen God face to face, and yet my life is preserved." (vv. 28–30)

Jacob has a new name. God has blessed him. He is still the trickster, of course. And though the God who wrestled with him blesses him, Jacob (now Israel) limps away from the riverside. Even when this God blesses us, our humanity remains a part of us.[34]

Afterthoughts

What have we learned? It is interesting to look at the list of metaphors and images and pictures that were assembled here. What kinds of tensions do we notice between them? Where are the similarities? To which are we drawn and attracted? Which offend us? What do we do with those that do not comfortably fit our understandings and experiences of God?

There are several interesting patterns in the almost sixty metaphors and pictures presented. What themes do you see? How, for instance, are "refuge," "fortress," "hiding place," and "shade" related? Why are there so many images that have to do with safety and hiding?

Are the metaphors used in the Psalms of lament different from those used in Psalms of thanksgiving and praise? They are most assuredly and understandably so. We use different names and paint different portraits of God depending on our lives and our living. What are the "relationship" metaphors? How are the parent/child, husband/wife, and shepherd/sheep metaphorical pairs different from other understandings of God?

Obviously all the metaphors and pictures discussed aren't of equal theological importance. Understanding God as the loving parent has far more potential to be expanded and explored than God as a moth or dry rot! And yet all of these images hold forth potential to shock or even entertain us, spurring thought and reflection, and ultimately understanding and knowing.

The dangers of our metaphorical language are clear. When God is imagined as father, fathers become gods. And yet without this metaphor, our theological reflections would be impoverished. We journey on, reading and listening and hoping that, in the end, our understandings of God and of ourselves will culminate in a world more just, more righteous, more compassionate. Always, that is the hope.

Questions for Reflection

Introduction: Questions to Use as You Begin

1. How were your own understandings of God formed and fashioned? How do we know what we know? Many have very early childhood memories of learning about God in worship, in Sunday school, or at home. Often parents or grandparents are pivotal in that what we know about God comes directly from what they have taught us, or indirectly from how they lived their lives.

2. What are your earliest memories of God language and of conversations about who and what kind of God we worship?

3. What are the favorite or most comfortable metaphors you use for God? In this volume we discuss many; some of them are familiar to you and some are not. Some are surprising and some may even be offensive. It will be interesting to explore these in conversation with others. Out of those conversations you will inevitably learn something about each other's lives, because our notions and understandings of God are formed not only by what others have told us but out of our life experiences as well. Our theologies are formed by the stories of our lives.

4. There are some important foundational questions to ask here. When you think about your own metaphors for God, are you envisioning a God who is very near, or far away? Is this a comforting God? Powerful? All-knowing? An intimate companion? Do you carry with you a different sense of God when you are suffering than when you are experiencing life's joys? How are these different and how are they the same?

5. Have there been times in your life when you have felt God's silence or absence? What was happening? What do you do to replenish or reconnect? What are your ways of seeking God?

Anointing One

1. The word anoint may be common in your tradition. In some traditions it is common, for instance, to talk about the anointing of the preacher. That may mean that the preacher at a certain point in time is blessed by the power of God's Spirit to bring an energized word, one that has great rhetorical power and force. Or the preacher is anointed to bring a prophetic word. That means that God's Spirit has enabled the preacher to bring a word that is challenging and difficult, one that the community may not want to hear, but that brings a cry for justice.

2. Once, a minister took from her purse a flask of oil. She dabbed a bit of oil on her finger and rubbed it on the forehead of the minister who was to preach that morning. In this way, she had given the preacher for the morning her special blessing. She then rubbed oil on the foreheads of the other ministers in the pulpit. This anointing served to bind the ministers together in solidarity around the task of preaching. They were to encourage the preacher of the morning with "Amens" and other signs of encouragement. To anoint is to empower and to encourage, as well as to bless and make special (or sacred).

   When I was diagnosed with a brain tumor a friend of mine who was a Roman Catholic priest met with me and after a prayer for healing put a small amount of oil on my forehead. He was drawing from the Catholic rite of "The Anointing of the Sick."

   Have you ever witnessed these kind of anointings or been part of an anointing ceremony? How were they alike or different from these? What were your own thoughts and feelings related to this ritual?

3. Some traditions would describe baptism as an anointing. What is your own understanding of baptism and that of your denomination or tradition? What did your own baptism mean to you and how does baptism anoint us for ministry in the world—all of us?

4. For what tasks have you been called? In what ways do you believe God gives you the confidence to carry them out?

5. What is the community's role in anointing people for their work in the world? In our worship, how do we acknowledge that what we do in our daily lives—as teachers, parents, secretaries, whatever—can be an avenue for God's redemptive work in the world?

Buckler (Shield)

1. Shield can have many meanings and can evoke different feelings. No one who is prepared for war would come to battle without armor or a shield to protect them. The buckler or shield provides protection from harm. We can think of physical shields; there are also invisible shields such as particular attitudes or spiritual resources that protect and sustain us. What are some of your spiritual resources?

2. Can you imagine a world where shields against violence, disappointment, or harm are not necessary?

3 Those of us who have lived any length of time know that God has not protected us from all illnesses, disappointments, or tragedies. You may have experienced the loss of a friend or family member; a sudden and unexpected divorce; abuse by a spouse, family member, or stranger; or a devastating illness. How do we think about these in relation to an understanding of God as shield, someone who protects us?

4. When have there been times when you wanted God to be a shield or take up a shield to defend you?

5. Perhaps you do not have an understanding of a God who defends and protects you. You have an understanding of a God, rather, who walks with you as you are experiencing your own devastations and grief. How do these different understandings influence how we pray or when we pray?

Cloud

1. Clouds are beautiful. They tell us something about what might happen next. Dark clouds signal that soon a heavy rain may fall. Big fluffy clouds delight and feed our imaginations.

   You might live in a place that on most days there is a cloudy sky or a constant fog that hangs over the city or countryside.

Or you might live in a dry, arid land that rarely experiences rain—only a drop or two, now and then, from a small cloud that quickly disappears from the sky. Where you live, what you have known, will influence how you think about God as cloud. If you live in the former, the cloud is the familiar and the known. If you live in the latter, the cloud provides the occasional respite from seemingly unending heat and blinding rays. The cloud is a sign of hope that, at least for a moment, the rain will come and replenish the dry ground. Life will be restored.

2. In the exodus story, the cloud provides guidance. The cloud is an indication that God is present in mysterious and powerful ways. When have you had this kind of experience of God—a mysterious one, perhaps a vision? Or, has God sent a message to you through another person or perhaps through something you have read? Did it provide direction when you had a life–changing decision to make? How do you know that what you heard is from God? How can we tell the voice of God from the other sounds, voices, and noises of the world?

Comforter

1. What faces come to mind when you think about the people who have sometime in your life comforted you? Perhaps you think of a trusted friend, a nurse, a pastor, a therapist, a teacher, or a relative such as a very special grandmother. The comforter understands our current distress and lends us hope.

2. The Old Testament is replete with stories and prophetic oracles about a God who is angry with God's people, but who, in the end, longs to restore relationship with them and calls them back "home." The book of Judges is about the Israelite people and how they repeatedly turned from God. Then, their enemies oppressed them. And then God sent a "judge," a leader, to restore them. The pattern was repeated again and again and again, but God never failed to deliver them. God as comforter is a God who knows that the people have somehow gone astray, but a God who also shows forgiveness. The people are restored and allowed the privilege of beginning life again; they are given a second chance.

In Isaiah 40 the word of comfort comes to an entire nation. "Comfort, O comfort my people" (v. 1), are the words of God to the prophet. The prophet is to bring a word of comfort to a people in exile. Think of times when your nation has needed comfort; your local community; your congregation. What words brought comfort to you?

3. For Third Isaiah the kind of comfort God provides is like the comfort that comes from a mother to her child: "As a mother comforts her child, / so I will comfort you" (66:13a). Mothers get angry at their children. And then, mothers restore relationship with them and long for them to have a good life.

When have you known this kind of comfort from God?.

Compassionate One

1. Compassion is to bear or suffer with someone or something. It is a stirring of the heart. A person who is truly compassionate cares without counting the cost. When have you felt God's presence as you have suffered during a time of loss or distress?

2. When have you been the compassionate one? What are the dangers and promises of showing compassion? Do you believe that God ever suffers as a result of showing compassion?

3. Some people say that they have the most profound sense of God's presence with them when they are feeling grief and despair. Some say that they have a profound sense of God's presence when they are filled with gratitude and joy at what life is sending them. When have you had your most intense and personal experiences of the presence of God?

4. One of the other translations of the Hebrew word usually translated "compassion" is "tender mercy." When have you known God's tenderness? In the Old Testament we are told that God has this kind of compassion for us. Sometimes the writer says this compassion is like that of a mother. Some say it is like that of a father. It is a reminder that either parent can have this "womblike," intimate kind of love for their children, just as God has that kind of love for each of us.

Creator

1. Experiences of the natural world can provide an awareness of the presence of God. A picture from the Hubble telescope, a view of the seemingly never-ending ocean, or a sunset that creates a sky of vivid orange are reminders of a powerful and creative God who has created the universe. Can you think of a time when you have had such an experience of awe and wonder?

2. That same experience can come when one first sees a newborn infant; this very small person captures all the complexities of the living human. We understand that in delicate and intricate ways this new person has been made. The affirmation that God has created us is attested to by the Psalms and by the prophets. Jeremiah, in relating the call to his ministry, says the word of the Lord came to him and said, "Before I formed you in the womb I knew you, / and before you were born I consecrated you..." Jeremiah speaks of a God who formed him and knows him.

   What does it mean to you that God knows you intimately? Is that a comforting thought? A frightening one?

3. Is the creator responsible for everything that comes into existence? If we are co-creators with God, then how do we share responsibility for what happens in our world? What are the most important things we are called to do? How do our church communities help us to do these things?

Dawn

1. Dawn symbolizes the breaking of light following the darkness of night. Dusk means that the light is waning. Soon the earth will rest. Michelangelo created two magnificent sculptures called "Dusk" and "Dawn. " They are turned in opposite directions, but they are alike. They often look alike, and they share this quality—we can count on them.

   The image of the dawn is intended to spark in readers' mind a connection to the steadfast quality of God's presence with us: never failing, constant, sure. Is that your experience of God? How do we talk about God's constant presence and, at the same time, also know of times when God seems to be silent or absent from us?

2. What can you count on? Who can you count on? What does it mean to think of God as steadfast and sure when life brings us so many upsets, disappointments, and challenges?

Deliverer

1. The Israelites knew God as the One who delivered them from slavery in Egypt. Have you experienced deliverance? From what have you been delivered? A fear? An addiction? Guilt? Gut-wrenching grief? Unsettling memories? Disease? Oppression? An enemy? What part has God played in your deliverance from these things?

2. In the Psalms, the speaker is often delivered from the "enemy." In the royal Psalms, those that describe the experiences of the king, the enemy is often a foreign nation or a foreign leader who threatens the welfare of the nation. But the enemy can be personal as well. How do nations, communities, or individuals become enemies? How can we intervene in the seemingly never-ending cycle in which violence is done to an enemy and then often returned in kind? How can we be delivered from our violence?

Dew

1. Often churches set aside a week or two out of the church year to hold a "revival." During this time it is hoped that, through worship, singing, preaching, and outreach to the community, the congregation will be restored and renewed. The congregation hopes that it will find new energy and once again become acquainted with its purpose and mission in the world. This is often a time when hope is restored, and the congregation wants to rekindle its commitment to establishing the realm of God on earth. Have you known such moments in your community's life when God's presence came upon you not in loud and thunderous ways, but in almost imperceptible and quiet ways?

2. "God as the morning dew"—this "picture" of God is a quiet, gentle one. God comes as silently as the dew comes upon the morning grass, providing life-giving and sustaining water for plants to survive. When have you felt this quiet, gentle presence of God fall gently upon you when you were in need of renewal and restoration? When you were in need of hope?

3. The hymn "Dear Lord, and Father of Mankind" by John G. Whittier talks about our "foolish ways" and expresses the desire that, somehow, in the midst of the chaotic lives that we create, we would find more simple, more calm ways to live. Verse 4 reads: "Drop thy still dews of quietness, till all our strivings cease; take from our souls the strain and stress, and let our ordered lives confess the beauty of thy peace."[1] The dew is not like a noisy rainstorm; it is not a flood. It is quiet. It is soft. It calms us in the midst of our storms. Has God brought you a calmness in the midst of stress?

Eagle

1. The eagle is often thought of as a symbol for the spirit and for wisdom, especially in native American and certain African cultures. In the United States, it is a symbol for strength. The eagle has keen sight. Its dwelling place is on high. It can soar and quickly dives earthward. The eagle lifts you up; it protects. The image of the eagle has been put to lyrics in the beloved hymn "On Eagles Wings," based on Psalm 91.

2. In Psalm 77 (vv. 16–20), the psalmist is recounting for the community one of the great deeds of God: the exodus and the passing of the Israelites through the Red Sea. With a poetic flourish the psalmist describes the waters of the sea and how they were afraid of the powerful God. It was a stormy day; water was pouring from the skies and there was lightning and thunder. Something important, colossal, was happening as the earth trembled. God led the people through the sea and away from the mighty Egyptians. The psalmist says, "Your way was through the sea, / your path, through the mighty waters; / yet your footprints were unseen" (v. 19).

This is the description of the "carrying" God. God, according to the psalmist, invisibly crossed with the people through the raging waters. Just as the mother eagle carries her young on her back through the skies, God had carried the people through the waters and then through the wilderness until they arrived at the Jordan River, the threshold to their new land.

When has God carried you through difficult and troubled times? Did God work through other people? Did God strengthen your own resiliency and give you courage to keep taking step after step? Were you inspired or encouraged through worship or through your relationships with your friends, family, or church community?

3. Once, when I was giving a lecture on different metaphors for God, I talked with a group of women and men about God as eagle—how in the Old Testament God as a mother eagle would spread her wings out over her young to protect them from harm. A person in the room responded that the image was suffocating to him! He did not like the thought of being covered by the wing, being in the dark and unable to move or fly! It was a good reminder that metaphors bring different thoughts, feelings, and responses depending on our life experiences and understandings.

Enemy

1. The word enemy is a negative one to us. The enemy is often one-dimensional in that we fail to see the good or the valued side of the contributions they make to the world. The enemy (such as the terrorist) can be seen as devoid of any good or redeeming feature. The enemy is "them" in contrast to "us." We then take up arms against them, aiming to prove only that we are right and good, while they are bad. Truth sways on the scaffold of falsehood. Seldom do we ask, "What can we learn about ourselves from our enemies?"

Perhaps, then, of all the "portraits" of God presented in this volume, "enemy" will be the most difficult for many. And yet, as we go about our day-to-day living, the understanding of God as the enemy, the one who does bad things to and against us is not so uncommon. It sneaks into our theological thinking in ways we are unaware.

When have you or someone you know asked: "Why did God do that to me? Why is God working against me? What have I done to deserve what God is doing? Am I being punished for the way I have lived my life?" These questions and their answers deserve some serious thinking and reflection. Are natural disasters a sign of God's wrath? Some well-known evangelists would have us believe that this is the case. They argued this in response to the destruction wrought by Hurricane Katrina on the United State's Gulf Coast. The hurricane, they said, was a sign that God was displeased with the way life was lived in New Orleans.

Is God the source of disaster and illness? A friend of mine, when first diagnosed with cancer, asked, "Why did God do this to me? I've lived life well. I have been faithful and good to others." She did not believe really in a God who inflicted the cancer cells on her, but in her time of worry and devastation, she reverted to a common theological affirmation: God brings our fortune and misfortunes, our illnesses and our good health. Does God do this? Why would God bring illness to some and not others?

2. The Israelites, when carried away from their own land to Babylon, thought of God as their enemy. It was God who had caused this to happen. Was it God? Was it the natural consequence of the ways they had lived life rather than the activity of God among them? Or was it the inevitable political development of a much larger and more powerful country, bent on expansion, conquering a much weaker neighbor?

Father

1. The term "father" is under reconstruction. It has a range of different meanings that cut across age, ethnicities, religious groups, cultures, and social classes. The media often play up the negative images of men being bad fathers. We need to look closely, then, at the father metaphor in the Old Testament.

There is a theme that runs loosely through the few texts in the

Old Testament that refer to God as father. It is this: The people have been unfaithful; they have been wrong. They cry out to a God who has been faithful and steadfast, and they are looking to a God who is their father who will forgive them, restore them, and refashion them into a faithful people. This is a picture of a faithful/loving parent and wayward, wandering children.

How is this understanding of God as one who forgives and restores your own understanding? Is this what comes to your mind when you think of God as father? What other associations are made with the use of the word father?

2. Is the understanding of God as father a primary one in your own church community? How is it used? When is it used?

3. What words come to mind when you describe your own father? How does this influence your own thinking about whether or not this is a helpful metaphor for God?

Father of Orphans

1. The word orphan conjures up countless scenes seen on the evening news. They are children whose parents have been killed or destroyed by AIDS, war, famine, and natural disasters. They are the children who have been left behind in a myriad of ways. They are the very young seen scrounging through piles of garbage searching for food or clothing or any means to survive. They are refugees. They are poor. The God who is the "father of orphans" reaches out to the impoverished, whatever form that poverty takes.

In the Old Testament, the orphans and the widows were the "lowest of the low." Because inheritance was passed through the male, the child without a father and the widow now without husband were left out of the "lines of power and wealth." They were the society's most vulnerable. Their fates and their well-being were left to fate; they depended on others for their recognition and survival. That is why the Old Testament prophets often framed their scathing indictments of the community around their abuse and neglect of the orphan and the widow. They symbolized those in need, those without, those who were often invisible to the wider community intent on accumulating their own wealth and good fortune.

The understanding of God as the "father of orphans," then, is a powerful one. It describes a God who is always looking out and caring for those without privilege, those who have been forgotten. How is this consistent with your own understanding of God? Is God a God of the poor and the voiceless?

2. If that is the case, then what does this mean to us who are trying to live out God's calling in the world? How is this compassionate perspective of a God who sees and empathizes with the destitute, who hears their cries, important for our own understanding of the mission of the church in a world whose landscape is scarred with strife, indifference, and apathy toward those in need?

Fire

1. The word fire can cause alarm and call forth horrid images. It can be a fear-filled word—we think of firebombs, the Holocaust (a word meaning: "massive destruction by fire") in Nazi Germany, a house unexpectedly ablaze. There are other more positive associations with the word fire—a campfire at the beach where stories are told and songs are sung, the warmth that comes from the wood stove in the winter.

The fire metaphor is equally multivalent. It symbolizes the call of Moses, God's guidance of the Israelites in the wilderness, the mysterious presence of God on the mountain. It can symbolize energy and light. When has your community felt "on fire"? Was God a part of your inspiration, your heightened motivation and resolve? What were the issues at stake? Did your community coalesce to achieve something or move past obstacles and barriers in your path?

2. When has a "fire," a disastrous situation or conflict, brought your attention or your congregation's attention to something important? Did it cause you to prioritize your resources, your time and energy and finances, in certain ways?

3. How have you felt God's Spirit and energy move within or among you in a fiery fashion?

Fortress

1. We don't very often talk about a "fortress" anymore. A fortress was the walled structure that stood between a person and the enemy. It kept certain people in and others out. Insiders were vulnerable to the world when they went outside their "fortress." Some of the cathedrals in Europe were built "fortress-like," God was seen as the fortress; God was invincible, unchangeable, the conqueror, the one who keeps us safe and secure from all harm.

2. How is the metaphor of "fortress" helpful to you? Have you known God to be a fortress at vulnerable times in your lives? Name some of those times.

3. What makes you comfortable with this understanding of God? Uncomfortable? How is this metaphor limited and what other metaphors are needed to complement it?

Friend

1. What does friend mean to you? How are friends different from the people who are mere acquaintances or familiar faces? How do friendships begin? How are they nourished?

2. Alice Walker one said, "No person is your friend (or kin) who demands your silence, or denies your right to grow and be perceived as fully blossomed as you were intended. Or who belittles in any fashion the gifts you labor so to bring into the world."[2] How is Walker's understanding of friendship a part of your own?

3. The rabbis who did the earliest interpretation on the Jewish Scriptures (the Old Testament) said, "Who is the mightiest of the mighty? The person who turns an enemy into a friend." How do you know that to be true? What stories do you know that demonstrate the power of "enemy turned friend"?

4. What does it mean to be a friend to God or for God to be a friend to you? How does this understanding fit with the understanding of God as creator or redeemer? When has your prayer life been "stilted" or awkward? When have you used language that was

formal, uncomfortable, or unfamiliar? When have you talked to God like you were talking to a friend across the table?

5. What are the strengths of this understanding? What are the limitations?

El Shaddai

1. If *El Shaddai* means "God of the breasts," it depicts a very intimate relationship between God and humanity: God as a nursing mother. Have you known intimate, loving moments with God? When? At the same time, *El Shaddai* is normally translated "God Almighty." This depicts a God who is all-powerful and strong. Do you hold both of these understandings of God? One more than the other? Do they contradict or do they complement each other?

2. *El Shaddai* can also mean God of the mountain. What have been some of your spiritual "mountaintop" experiences?

3. In the stories related to *El Shaddai* in Genesis, people often get new names. Abram's name is changed to Abraham. Jacob's name is changed to Israel. How did you get your name? If you were to give yourself a name that reflects the person you are today, what would it be?

Healer

1. Have you known someone who was miraculously healed, or have you yourself experienced a miraculous healing from a physical ailment or disease? What were the circumstances of that healing? Why do you think some people are healed from disease but some are not? Is healing a sign of God's favor?

2. Psalm 41 begins with a beatitude and offers a very interesting perspective on healing. What do you think about the psalm's first three verses? "Happy [Blessed] are those who consider the poor; / the Lord delivers them in the day of trouble. / The Lord protects them and keeps them alive; / they are called happy in the land... / The Lord sustains them on their sickbed; / in their illness you heal all their infirmities."

3. Have you been a part of a church community that needed healing? What kinds of things happened that allowed healing to take place?

4. What in our nation needs healing? What would a nation that lives in covenant with God look like? Sound like? What kinds of relationships would it have to other nations in the world?

Helper

1. As you think back over your life, who have been your helpers? Who are the people who have supported you and who have, during times of crisis, brought you insight, courage, and hope?

2. For whom have you been the helper?

3. When you think about God as helper, what times in your life come to mind? How has God helped you? Were you aware at the time that God was working through your life? Or, was it only in retrospect that you became aware that God had been with you?

4. Have there been times when you were troubled or worried but could not or did not cry out for help?

Hiding Place

1. Did you play "hide and seek" as a child? What are your memories? Did you stick out a toe, make a noise, rustle the curtain so that someone would find you? When in your life did you want to hide so that no one could find you? Were you afraid or ashamed?

2. How is God a place to hide? What does this mean to you? Is God a momentary place to find respite from an otherwise chaotic world? Do you sense a place that is quiet and secluded? Something else?

Holy One

1. When have you been most aware of your lack of perfection, the ways you are not like the God who called and named you?

2. How do we, aware of our own sinfulness, move and grow into being more like this holy God? What does it mean to be "of God" in a world that often is not? Our answers to what might be considered holy behavior, motives, attitudes, and lifestyles might vary. But to be holy—of the sacred—requires intentionality and a life of prayer and of study. That is what we sing about in the well-known hymn "Take Time to Be Holy":

    > Take time to be holy, speak oft with they Lord;
    >   abide in him always, and feed on his word.
    > Make friends of God's children; help those who are weak;
    >   forgetting in nothing God's blessing to seek.[3]

    Even in this hymn there are different thoughts and ideas about how one might go about living the holy life: prayer, studying the word of God, being friends with all of God's children, helping those who are vulnerable, and seeking God's presence and blessing. Which of these are priorities for you when you think about your own understanding of discipleship?

Hunter

1. There are places in the Old Testament where the compassionate God calls out to a wayward Israelite community, and with the love of the most caring parent, calls them home. Christian communities often sing of the Jesus who softly and tenderly calls the sinner to "come home," to come back to the God who loves them.

    Hosea describes a God who more aggressively seeks out the people who have not been faithful to the covenant. This is the God who goes out, net in hand, to find the people, gather the people, and bring them back. What kind of responses do you have to this more angry, assertive kind of God who will do anything to call people back to a way of living that has the potential to be rich, fruitful, and abundant?

Husband

1. This metaphor, as much as any in this volume, causes us to ask some important questions. What are the limitations of our

metaphorical language for God? How are metaphors "bound" by the time and place in which they were written? Can we simply take and appropriate an understanding of God that was acknowledged and affirmed in a place very different from own? What are the dangers inherent in using metaphorical language for God?

2. How comfortable are we with an angry God? Are there things that happen in this world that we would desperately want God to be angry at? Is that better than believing in a God who doesn't see or doesn't respond to the oppressive and violent ways of our world?

In the scenarios described in this entry, God as the jealous husband is angry. Then, in Isaiah and Hosea, the angry God turns compassionate. The anger melts into a longing to have the people back in relationship once again.

Judge

1. Have there been times in your life when the primary metaphor or understanding of God of your community was that of "judge"? What are your memories of understanding God as the one who keeps a careful accounting of what you have done wrong, your sins and transgressions?

2. How is the understanding of God as judge in this volume like or not like your own understanding of God as judge? What are the differences and why are they important?

3. Do you have an understanding of a God who responds to the wayward or ungodly ways of the world in which live? How do we know what is godly and what is not when different church communities hold varied and sometimes contradictory understandings?

Leopard, Lion, Mother Bear

1. These animal metaphors depict a God who wants desperately to find a people who have wandered away. There are other metaphors in the Old Testament that depict the same kind

of God and divine activity. Yet, these metaphors may bring a kind of discomfort that the others do not. What are your own responses to Hosea's use of the leopard, lion, and mother bear? Read Hosea 13:1—8. Why is God angry? Why does God feel forsaken after all God has done for the covenant people?

Light

1. At what times in your life have you known God as one who shines light upon your path to give you clarity or insight?

2. When have you known God to bring light into your experience of the "dark night of the soul"—a time when you were wrestling, anxious, or depressed?

3. When has scripture been the light on the path?

Maggots, Moths, Rottenness

1. These metaphors speak of a God who eats away at what is unrighteous or sinful. It portrays a God who eats away at what is "not right." Think about this understanding of God on the varied levels of life.

2. What needs to be "eaten away" in our nation? Are there practices, understandings, priorities that need to be destroyed so that we have a more peaceful, productive existence?

3. What needs to be "eaten away" in your church community? Are there practices or understandings that keep your community from living out the gospel in the wider community where you are located? What are your road blocks or obstacles to thriving and bringing the realm of God to those around you?

4. What needs to be "eaten away" or destroyed in your own life so that you can live more productively, creatively, and abundantly? What do you need to cast aside?

Midwife

1. The Old Testament gives witness to a God who is with us in the womb and as we are being birthed. What are your earliest memories of God and of God's care? Do you have early memories

of worship? How are they formative in your own current understandings of how God works in the world?

2. The passage from Isaiah above speaks about a God who is with us at childhood and then all through our lives—even until we have gray hair. Is this consistent with your own understandings, thoughts, and feelings? Do you look back on your life and see God's consistent and persistent presence? Has your spiritual journey been more checkered and spotty?

3. What are the stories you carry within you that give witness to God's never-failing care?

Mother

1. Do you know stories about your birth? What are they? What have you been told?

2. What words come to mind when you think of your mother? Or when you are asked what it means to be "motherly"?

3. When in your life did you begin to think about God as "mother"? Is this an important understanding for you? How does the language in your own church community/congregation support understandings of God as mother? How important is it to recognize that the biblical writers thought of God in this way?

4. That the mother metaphor has gained acceptance and is meaningful to many is demonstrated by the many contemporary hymns that depict God as mother. Often these are offered in parallel with father metaphors. Do you use these hymns in your worship? When do the authors of the hymn's words describe mother and father in ways that challenge our society's stereotypes of what it means to be male or female?

My Chosen Portion/My Cup

1. Are there times when you have chosen to be in relationship with God? Times you have not? What was happening in your life that encouraged you to make one decision or the other?

2. Read Psalm 73 and Psalm 142. What do you think it means that God is known to the psalmist as "my portion"?

Parent

1. How do you think the metaphor of God as parent is a helpful or an important one?

2. The Old Testament uses the metaphor to depict a God who is invested in and vulnerable to God's children. If you are a parent, what do you know about this investment and vulnerability?

3. How does your perspective of the metaphor change when you remember your days as a child? Were you a wanderer? Were there times that you turned away from your parents and then longed to return?

Potter

1. How has God fashioned and refashioned your life?

2. The image of the potter speaks of God's ability to sit "at the wheel" and create and then re-create us anew. It speaks of God's ability to take something that is flawed and start again. It speaks of second chances and of God's ability to keep working until something beautiful is created. How do you know this kind of God?

3. Pottery once dried in the kiln can be easily broken. How do we as earthen treasures know this kind of fragility?

> Have thine own way, Lord! Have thine own way!
> Thou art the potter; I am the clay.
> Mold me and make me after thy will,
> while I am waiting, yielded and still.[4]

When have you been able to speak these words...and mean them?

Following is a prayer of Irenaeus, a second-century theologian. Think about his words.

> Since you are the work of God, wait patiently for the hand of your Artist, who does all things at the right time. Present to him a supple and docile heart, and keep the form that this Artist gave you, having in yourself the water that comes from him and without which you would become hard and would reject the imprint of his fingers. By letting yourself

be formed by him, you will rise to perfection, for through this art of God, the clay that is in you will be hidden; his hand created your substance... But if you become hard and push away his art and show that you are discontent with the fact that he made you a human being, by your ingratitude towards God you will have rejected not only his art but life itself; for it is the very nature of God's goodness to form, and to be formed is the very nature of being human. Thus, if you give yourself to him by giving him your faith in him and your submission, you will receive the benefit of his art and you will be God's perfect work. If on the contrary, you resist him and if you flee from his hands, the cause of your incompleteness will be in yourself who did not obey, and not in him.[5]

Prosecutor

1. When have you felt like you were "on trial"?

2. When have you been exposed to understandings of God as a prosecutor bringing a long list of accusations?

3. When have you felt that you haven't lived up to God's expectations? How do we know what God wants and needs from us? How is being in a faith community helpful in your own discernments?

4. What do you think of the answer Micah gives to the question about God's requiring justice, kindness, and walking with humility? What do these three things mean to you?

   Who have you known who embodies these qualities?

Protector of Widows

1. The laws in Deuteronomy demonstrated that there were people in society who needed special attention and protection. Repeatedly, the laws call attention to the stranger, the widow, and the orphan as those who need care. In the Psalms, God is named as the protector of the widow, and we are called also to be the protectors of those in need. Who in your community is particularly vulnerable to oppression and harsh treatment? Who in our global community?

2. In many societies, women are struggling to gain the right to be recognized and heard. In what parts of the world are women particularly oppressed? What do you know about efforts to help them? What are the services provided for women in your town or city? How can you help the women who have no one to support them?

Redeemer

1. Redemption involves being drawn out of one world and into another. When have you been drawn out of a world of guilt into a world of forgiveness? Out of a world of fear into courage? Out of oppression into resistance?

2. When have you been a redemptive force in someone else's life—helping them to see new possibilities and live into them? Who have been the redemptive forces in your own life?

3. Many of our Christian hymns refer to redemption as that which happens when our earthly lives are over and we are ushered into eternity. We sing that Jesus has made this possible for us. A good example of this is in "Praise Him! Praise Him!"

   Praise Him! praise him! Jesus, our blessed Redeemer!
   Sing, O Earth, his wonderful love proclaim!
   Hail him! hail him! Highest archangels in glory;
   strength and honor give to this holy name!...
   Praise him! praise him! Jesus our blessed Redeemer!
   For our sins he suffered, and bled and died;
   he our Rock, our hope of eternal salvation,
   hail him! hail him! Jesus the crucified.[6]

   But the Old Testament understanding of redemption is something much more "of this earth." We are redeemed and ushered out of old ways and into the new over and over again in our lives.

Refuge

1. Psalm 91 has been taken to the battlefield by those who are fearful for their lives. What is your own understanding of war, of God being on one side or the other?

2. What is your own thinking about God's protection? Does God protect us from harm? How does God work in our world in the midst of evil and danger and suffering?

3. Read Psalms 61—64. This collection of songs has a strong theme of God's watchful oversight and care. When have you known or felt God's care? When have you looked back on life events and realized that God was with you, though you had not been aware of that presence when the experiences were happening to you?

4. What does it mean to you and your community to be "refuged" in God?

5. In Christian communities we sing, "O God, our help in ages past, our hope for years to come, / our shelter from the stormy blast, and our eternal home!"[7] What have been your life storms?

Rock

1. The well-known hymn, "Rock of Ages," begins this way: "Rock of Ages, cleft for me, let me hide myself in thee..."[8]) When have you known God to be the place that you could go for quiet, respite, a break from life's unexpected or harsh demands?

2. When have you felt yourself on solid ground, emboldened, and courageous because God was the foundation on which you stood?

Salvation

1. Over the years, what has been your own understanding of the word salvation? Or "being saved"? From what were you saved? What has been your understanding of the relationship between salvation, faith, grace, and heaven?

2. What is your own understanding of having "abundant life"? How do you experience that yourself or in your community?

3. Read some of the appeals for salvation that the psalmists lift up to God in Psalms 3:7; 6:4; 7:1; 12:1; 20:9; 22:21; 28:9; 31:16; 54:1; 59:2; 60:5; 69:1; 71:2; 86:2; 106:47; 108:6; 109:26; 118:25; 119:94. When have you known such urgency and desperation?

Shade/Shadow

1. Picture yourself under the branches of a great and mighty tree on a very hot, scorching day. What kind of relief do the limbs provide? How is God this kind of presence in our lives?

Shepherd

1. Is the Twenty-third Psalm associated with any important and meaningful occasions in your life—a funeral, wedding, baptism, or ordination?

2. What do you know about the life of the shepherd and the relationship between the sheep and their shepherd?

3. When have you known God to be a gathering God, a God who gathers people back and into community, just as the shepherd gathers his sheep?

4. Sometimes in the Old Testament the Israelites are compared to "sheep without a shepherd." What images does this phrase conjure in your mind? When have you thought that your own church community could be described this way?

Shower

1. Have you ever lived in a drought-ridden area? How did the experience emphasize the importance of water?

2. The people of Israel were dependent on rainfall for their food, for their lives. What Old Testament stories do you associate with drought?

3. What are your favorite biblical passages that refer to water, streams, rivers, or thirst? Have you known dire thirst? Have you ever had a thirst for God? How does the metaphor of rain speak a word of hopefulness to those who are thirsty for God?

Song

1. Have their been times in your life when you have known God as "your song"? When were those times? What was happening?

2. In Old Testament texts sometimes "song" is paired with "strength." "The Lord is my strength and my [song]..." How do these two words work together in your life experience?

3. Have there been times in your life when you did not feel like singing? What helped you move toward hopefulness or joy? How was the community important in this process? Prayer?

4. When have you known God to have voice or "sing" through someone you know?

Stronghold of the Oppressed

1. The Old and New Testaments bear witness to a God who wants bonds broken and the oppressed to go free. In your lifetime, what are the amazing global stories of liberation and redemption?

2. Have you known oppression? How does God work through the world and its people to bring an end to all our oppressions?

3. Have you been an agent of liberation and reconciliation? Did you speak when a freeing, affirming word needed to be spoken?

4. What are your favorite spirituals? How do they speak to this understanding of God who is the stronghold for oppressed peoples?

Suffering One

1. There are different understandings of evil and suffering in relation to God. What we say to those who are suffering often carries with it theological understandings and ideas that we have not carefully analyzed. For instance, when we say to someone who is suffering, "God doesn't give you more than you can handle," we are saying that God has somehow "sent" the suffering to the one in pain.

   Or when we say that a person who has faith will be healed, we are, at the same time, saying that those who remain ill, or even die, have not had enough faith. These are important things to think about in any community of faith.

2. Many of the Old Testament writers had an understanding that suffering was a punishment from God. Have you ever received or sent that message? How do you hold this understanding in tension with the idea that God is a God of love and grace?

3. While evil and suffering are present in the world, some argue that they are not sent by God, but that God is present as we

experience them and endure. Have you known the presence of God in times of challenge and suffering? How was that presence manifest—through an inner but unexplained peacefulness, through the kindness and support of someone: a friend, a stranger, or a family member?

4. What is your own understanding of how God works in the world in relation to sickness or natural disasters?

Sun

1. How is your experience of God like the sun coming up over the horizon at daybreak?

2. How is your experience of God like the intense light that comes from the sun at midday?

3. Have you ever had an experience when the light of day dispelled fears or doubts?

4. Has God's presence caused light to shine on the pathway so that your decisions became more focused and clear?

Sustainer

1. What sustains you? How do you keep the energy and persistence to "keep on keeping on"?

2. What is the relationship between sustenance and hope?

3. Are you a resilient person? Where does resiliency come from? Is it born within us? Does the strength to endure come from God?

4. Who are the sources of support and encouragement in your life? Whom do you support and encourage?

The One Who Lifts My Head

1. This is an infrequently used but beautiful picture of God and God's working in our lives.

What causes someone to lower his or her head? Guilt, shame, embarrassment, depression, fatigue, hopelessness, a lack of self-esteem or worth? How is God active in our world providing what people need to look up and face the world? Forgiveness to replace guilt or shame? Hope to counter hopelessness? An understanding that each person is a beloved child of God to counter doubts about worthiness and acceptability?

Vineyard Owner

1. God invests in us much like the gardener invests time and energy in the planting and harvesting of crops. How has God invested in you? What opportunities have been given you?

2. The poem of the vineyard in Isaiah 5 suggests that, though God had invested in the people, God was disappointed in the crop's yield. God saw violence and the cries of the oppressed. When God looks at our world as we are living it, what do you believe would be God's greatest disappointments? In your church community, your neighborhoods, our nation, the world?

Voice

1. Have you heard God's voice? Some people describe spectacular visions and voices they believe to be God's way of encouraging or guiding them. Some describe gentle nudgings throughout their lives conveying God's urgings and longings for our living.

   How do we know that the whispers or shouts are from God? In the midst of all the noise of the world, how do we know when we are being faithful?

Warrior

1. Are you a pacifist? Do you believe that there is cause for "just war"? Are there things God would want us to fight for even if it meant loss of life, even the loss of innocent lives?

2. In times of war, nations believe that God is on "their side." How have you seen this played out in the history of our own nation?

3. Some communities will no longer sing "Onward Christian Soldiers" because of its militaristic imagery. If it is time to give up the image of God as warrior, is there a metaphor that can

replace it—one that demonstrates God's willingness to engage the world to break down oppressive structures and put in place new ones?

Wrestler

1. In Genesis, Jacob wrestles with God. Have you ever wrestled with God? What is the story of your wrestling?

2. How do you equate wrestling with God with matters of conscience and with an innate sense of wanting to do "what is right"?

Metaphors and Ministry
The Skyline Has Changed:
A Big Tree Has Fallen

DR. ARCHIE SMITH JR.

*"Metaphor consists in giving the thing a name that belongs
to something else; the transference being either from genus to
species or from species to species or on the grounds of analogy"*—
Aristotle[1]

Many metaphors are regular parts of our lives: "The jig is up!
She turned the question over in her mind. Time is money. Sheila
is a lioness in battle. John's anger was hot as fire. She is green with
envy. God is father. Jesus is the lamb that was slain. The chairperson
ploughed through the agenda. She was tore up from the floor up.
Life is a journey. Are you standing in harm's way?"

By what metaphors do we live? What is "meta" for? Its power to
transform meaning has long been noted in politics, literature, religion,
and human communication in general. We cannot understand our
world apart from metaphor or figurative speech. Preachers who
interpret texts and human lives may hold a special interest in the
use and power of metaphor to communicate the meaning of God's
word for our lives today. Preachers may be interested in more than
"giving the thing a name," as Aristotle suggested. Preachers may be
interested in how metaphor aids in the interpretation of meaning
and enables individuals and communities to understand how God
is at work in the world today.

My seminary homiletics professor, an influential teacher,
theologian, and pastor, recently died. He was age ninety-three at the
time of his death. He had just finished volume one of a two-volume

work. He became ill and never recovered. Many of his former students attended his memorial service. One student said, "He was a blessing to us all." We wondered how to find the right words, the big words, to express his impact upon our lives and show our gratitude. The minister who gave the eulogy found words to state what we were feeling. He used several metaphors to capture the complexity and state the heart of the matter. "The skyline has changed," he said. "A big tree has fallen!" The preacher created a tension in our minds between the changed skyline, the fallen big tree, and our "fallen" professor. New meaning began to emerge.

Some big trees fall easily because they have shallow roots. When a strong windstorm blows through they fall. But this big tree was different. Its roots were deep and it knew how to endure. We, his students, came to expect our professor to be there. When he died, when the big tree fell, the skyline had indeed changed. Metaphor was a way to speak about our teacher's life and death, and its meaning for us.

The skyline is the horizon where earth and sky meet. The skyline of a city, for example, helps us to know where we are. We can see the outline of buildings or mountain range. Each city has its own unique skyline, its own organization and way of standing out against the background of the sky. My homiletics professor encouraged us to develop and value our own unique gifts for preaching and to aim high, just as he did. The one who gave the eulogy used metaphor to put in perspective the blessing his life and teaching had been to us.

"The skyline has changed." "A big tree has fallen!" The familiar, taken-for-granted world that we have always known has now forever changed. The fallen tree has created a big gap, a noticeable void. Things are forever changed. Something new and yet unknown to us will, someday, grow in its place.

Metaphor is indispensable to preaching. It is a way of stating something that is unfamiliar, complex, confusing, and strange (e.g., the absence of our renowned teacher and beloved friend) by using language that is a familiar part of everyday life ("the skyline") .

Metaphor makes things accessible by bringing them within reach. Metaphor, then, extends the range of the meaning of things and empowers us to make sense of our own experiences in its light. It can orient and help us to know where we have been and where we may be heading. The past, present, and future can be connected or extended through the use of metaphor. Our understanding of things may be placed in a certain perspective, and we may find a helpful context for interpreting our experiences. Choices may be opened and new possibilities for relationships and action may arise because metaphor has enabled us to see further and know differently.

This is what Mary Donovan Turner does in this wonderfully accessible volume. Metaphors for God enable us to see something about our world and the Divine that we had not seen before. We come to appreciate how metaphor can help us see the extraordinary in ordinary, everyday experiences, in ways similar to our biblical forbearers. Our hearts tremble when we see God's presence in ordinary experience.

Metaphor in Religious Life

What is "meta" for? Ian G. Barbour helps us with an understanding of the role of metaphor in religious life. Metaphors function as a bridge between the familiar world and a new, emerging world, between human activity and God's on-going creativity. Metaphor is the language of transition. It helps us to see the emerging, new, and unfamiliar in the light of the old and familiar. "Meta" is for helping to see above and beyond conventional views. What helps the metaphor work or hold relevance is the tension between the two worlds (the old and the new). Hence, "Metaphor," Barbour says, "proposes analogies between the normal context of a word and a new context into which it is introduced."[2] In so doing, metaphor can order our perception and thinking, inform our attitudes and behaviors as we contemplate one thing in the light of another. The metaphor is transitory in that it is a bridge, but not a model for the new experience. Models endure, but metaphors are temporary constructs to help inform our models. The metaphor cannot be taken literally. It is often understood as a figure of speech, multivalent and open to a variety of interpretations. Barbour gives an example of someone who may feel sad and say, "My heart is heavy." This is not to be taken literally and, therefore, we are not to take out a scale and weigh the heart. Rather, it is a poetic and graphic way to understand what we cannot see (God, spirit, the emotions, belief, meaning, or interpretation) and understand these in the light of what we can grasp: something that is heavy, burdensome, exacting. It may call for a range of responses, an opportunity to help or motivate the opposite, an opportunity to take advantage. The meaning of the response depends upon the context.

Metaphor in Literature and Philosophy

George Lakoff asks important questions, such as, "What is reason?" and, "How do we make sense of our experience?" In order to address these important questions, he defines metaphor as imaginative language based on experience. "Meta" is for assisting our thinking about things in our world. Metaphor is an important aspect of reason; it is mental imagery that enables us to go beyond particular physical limitations of our world, to make sense of or explore the meaning of our experience. Metaphor, according to Lakoff, is a form of abstraction in that the metaphor itself is not embodied or located as a physical entity. It does not "correspond to anything that exists independent of human conceptual systems."[3]

According to Lakoff and Johnson, metaphors are an integral part of everyday life, influencing not only what we say, but what we think and how we behave: "What we experience, and what we do everyday is very much a matter of metaphor."[4] These authors provide an example of how metaphor structures the way we see, think, and act in the world. The metaphor "argument is war" provides the language we use, the way we think about an argument, and how we behave. We defend our position, attack our opponent, demolish or shoot down his or her argument. Our goal is to win, not lose, the argument. Our entire approach is structured in terms of a battlefield, a war zone. But if we used a different metaphor, our way of seeing, thinking, and behaving might be entirely different—so might we, and our world.

The ideas of defending, attacking, and shooting down the opponent's argument might be irrelevant if we used a different metaphor. Consider the idea of argument as a dance. Now "the participants are seen as performers, and the goal is to perform in a balanced and aesthetically pleasing way. In such a culture, people would view arguments differently, experience them differently, carry them out differently, and talk about them differently."[5] These authors' big point is that metaphor is not mere words or fancy speech, but a way of re-envisioning the world in ways that guide what we see, how we think, and what we do. "The essence of metaphor," then, "is understanding and experiencing one kind of thing in terms of another."[6]

Emotions, ideas, and happenings that are a part of our experience are not often clearly presented. We may be confused or disoriented. We may need the help of other, familiar ideas from a previous time to get a hold on confusing ideas, beliefs, or emotions in order to better understand what is going on in the here and now. Metaphor may play this role. In this way, metaphor is potentially revolutionary, especially when we consider that the metaphors we live by are based in the rough-and-tumble self-experiences of everyday life. They may serve as a bridge between past memories and present construing.

Multivalent metaphors suggest the complexity of our experiences with many and different values and meanings that may be contradictory and paradoxical. Multivalent metaphors are the mental scaffolds that can contribute to change—a conversion experience, a paradigm shift—or result in transforming our worldview. Metaphors may also serve to frighten and paralyze action—e.g., the dark of midnight will swallow you up! Multivalent metaphor may serve to move us forward or backward depending upon the context and the uses to which metaphorical communication is put. The choice of a metaphor and recognition of its possibilities and limits, as Turner points out, is crucial.

How Does Metaphor Relate to Theology?

Sallie McFague, in her two books *Metaphorical Theology* and *Speaking in Parables*,[7] brings theology back to its metaphorical roots and argues that metaphors are significantly helpful in enabling Christian theologians to work in our present context. According to McFague, the purpose of theology is to help make it possible for the gospel to be heard in our time.[8] Is religious language still meaningful, or has it become hopelessly irrelevant? When religious language becomes literal or exclusive, then the possibility of hearing the "good news" is deadened because it is no longer new or good.

John Hick argues the relevance of metaphor for doing Christian theology in *The Metaphor of God Incarnate*. He examines a core Christian theological conviction—namely, the Incarnation. How do we talk in finite terms about "the infinite transcendent reality that we call God"[9]? Isn't this a contradiction? Isn't all human language about the divine reality a limited human creation and, therefore, inadequate? This is precisely Hick's point. There are radically and incompatible different points of view among Christians concerning this particular multivalent theological metaphor. Incarnation

> ...is the product of devout and faithful men and women... some of them extremely intelligent and thoughtful and others less so, who were, like everyone else, enabled and yet also limited by the presuppositions and cognitive resources of a particular time and place. One can usually tell from their way of thinking to what period and sub-traditions they belonged. And because theology is a human artifact, it has changed almost out of recognition as the circumstances of human life have changed. Ideas which at one time seemed self-evident or divinely authorized have sometimes come in a different age to seem implausible or even offensive.[10]

Hick demonstrates how a particular metaphor can be put to radically different and incompatible use. Here he uses metaphor to talk about the Incarnation in a way that takes historical experience into account. As we shall see, there are many different controversial responses to the meaning of this theological metaphor. Hicks identifies six controversial responses to the Incarnation metaphor. I present them briefly here. (1) God is involved in everyday human life and history. Both history and everyday life are important to God. God is Immanuel, God with us. Most every major religious tradition affirms the presence and participation of the divine Other in human affairs. The controversy here may be that Christianity is not a unique, superior religion, but one religious tradition among many. (2) God is not only involved in human life generally, but specifically, particularly and effectively in the life of Jesus. God was present in Jesus in an extraordinary way and this "extraordinary way" has universal significance for the way we live our lives today. The controversy here is that Jesus is God's special revelation to humankind. To know God in the special way is to come through Jesus. (3) This third point directs our focus to the *pre-existence* of Jesus as the starting point for understanding the Incarnation. In this way, it "takes a major step beyond the previous two" positions, and trumps other religious claims. The controversy is that this claim makes Jesus a divine being, the only begotten of God. Therefore other religions are inferior to Christianity. (4) The fourth position suggests that there is "a total interaction of the divine and the human in Christ." God completely empties the divine-self in Jesus. Hence, Jesus is fully God and fully human at the same time. The controversies are many. How can the infinite be completely located in finite time and space—in the life of Jesus? This belief, like the one before it, subordinates all religious claims but its own. (5) A fifth position holds that God's Incarnation in Jesus is the only divine incarnation and no other full incarnation will come. "The 'incarnation' in this fifth view means that Christ is in a category distinct from all other forms of revelation."[11] A controversial point is that the revelation in Jesus is exclusive and final. (6) Finally, the incarnate Jesus is physically, substantively, different from all other humans. The language to describe this is from the Council of Chalcedon (451 C.E.). Jesus, the incarnate one, is truly God and truly human. He is like us in all respects, yet without sin. Is this to be understood literally? The controversy centers on how this language is compatible with postmodern understandings of God and humankind.[12]

Sally McFague tells us that the purpose of theology is to make it possible for the gospel to be heard in our time and that metaphor is central to this purpose. In John Hick's work, we can see how a single multivalent theological metaphor can point in radically different and incompatible directions. Multivalent theological metaphors point to very different belief systems and ways of being in the world. This suggests the idea that there may be more than one "Christianity."

In a parallel way, Turner shows us how "moth" and "maggot" were once used as multivalent metaphors for the Divine in biblical times. Those metaphors arose from the common and everyday experiences of the people. They were in conventional use at the time, but today no one uses the language of "moth" or "maggot" as metaphor for the Divine reality. This suggests that when certain practices and patterns of experiences die, so do the metaphors that arose from them. How are we to think about God as the abusive husband or God as warrior? Have the need and the contexts for these metaphors "died" so that they no longer serve us well?

The question remains—How can we communicate meaningfully about the infinite Divine presence and activity by using finite categories, entities, or limited experiences? In which ways and contexts are metaphors for the Divine appropriate and illuminating? In which ways are they inappropriate and misleading? How can culturally bound metaphors open us to fresh metaphors for the Divine in our day?

There is always a deeper reality that operates below the surface of whatever it is that we are doing or contemplating. There is always more going on than what we can see, or grasp, cognitively. Metaphor can help us to appreciate the complexity of any moment or experience, especially when we understand the context and historical forces that give them rise.

It is important to state that each new generation of Christian believers is challenged to find language that enables it to talk about complexity, the unfamiliar, and the unknown. The mystery of the Incarnation is just one example that challenges us to interpret the complexity of Christian traditions in contemporary experiences. We might ask, "How does Generation X talk about or evaluate incarnational experiences?" What language does it use to communicate about the unfamiliar and unknown, the uncanny, and experiences of awe? If it is the case that all human communication is fraught with metaphorical meaning, then how will Generation X, for example, address the controversies of pluralism similar to what John Hicks mentioned above? How might their interpretation of Incarnation in Christian traditions or religious experiences challenge or be challenged by the emerging new Christianity, the new rise of evangelical Christians on the right or on the left, progressive Christianity, prosperity gospel? Sallie McFague is right: metaphors are vital to theological interpretation because they operate on the imaginative level to generate new meaning, extend, and guide, thus challenging our fundamental way of seeing something unfamiliar, thereby changing our relationship to it.

Metaphors in Preaching and Pastoral Care

Pastoral care is a dimension of practical theology and it begins with experience and with the recognition that not all of experience is in conscious awareness. Pastoral care may begin with a call for assistance or be initiated by a recognized need. Pastoral care providers are challenged to listen on several different levels simultaneously: the emotional and unconscious, cognitive, behavioral, and relational. These levels are always contextualized by certain economic, political, and structural realities. Pastoral care providers also pay close attention to detail and to how the contexts and interpretations help to shape the meaning of whatever is happening. These challenges are no less for the preacher or interpreter of texts. Both the preacher and the pastoral care provider are interpreters of sacred written texts and living human documents. And they must remain alert to the question, "What is God doing through the shaping influences of history and contemporary experiences?" Metaphor and the uses of language and action are crucial resources for the preacher and pastoral care provider's common interpretive tasks.

Pastoral psychotherapists are also interested in the unconscious and how metaphor works. Metaphor may be used to caution, encourage, inspire, suggest solutions to problems, help people to recognize themselves, seed ideas and increase motivation, or to reframe situations.[13] An individual, for example, "may take a metaphor literally on the conscious level, while on the unconscious level perceiving its symbolic meaning."[14] The pastoral psychotherapist can use metaphorical communication to attribute meaning, foster change, create tension between points of view and offer choice that may lead to new ways of acting.

The metaphors we live by help to settle what we see, know, and do. I suggest two ecological or systemic metaphors: the metaphor of the web,[15] and the metaphor of the river.[16] Of course, there are others. Both are ecological metaphors with contemporary relevance.

They can help us to interpret our common life in terms of wholes: to view the self as relational, a part of a network that includes nature, to track the connection between things, and to appreciate reciprocal influences. Both the web and river metaphors provide us with contemporary imagery for God, Spirit *and* world as interrelated, and are creative in ways that make them similar to metaphors our biblical ancestors used.

Web of Life Metaphor

The following words were attributed to Chief Seattle in 1854: "Man did not weave the web of life—he is merely a strand in it. Whatever he does to the web, he does to himself."[17] The web, in this statement, points to the interrelatedness of all things. A more contemporary version of this may be found in the words of Martin Luther King Jr.: "We are caught in an inescapable network of mutuality, tied in a single garment of destiny. Whatever affects one directly affects all indirectly."[18] The web imagery also finds resonance in Ephesians 4:25. "We are members of one another." All the metaphors in this book presuppose a fundamental relation between God, the covenant, and community. They presuppose a web and weavers of the web. Everything is related to the divine reality. Such metaphors as "potter," "mother/woman giving birth," "protector of widows," "stronghold of the oppressed," or, "the one who lifts my head" are relational metaphors suggesting the many ways in which the divine reality is experienced in everyday life. How, then, do we talk about our self-relatedness and relations to one another with moral responsibilities? The idea that our lives are interconnected, that we are co-creators of our co-emerging world, that what we do to others has consequences for the becoming of ourselves may be hard to see or affirm in a materialistic, prosperity-oriented culture of hyper-individualism. Our fundamental interrelatedness may be hard to see in a society that obscures the real and reciprocal connections between individuals, class, cultures, and genders.

A popular and fast-growing charismatic movement within professing Christianity in recent years involves the "prosperity gospel." It is not a new denomination, but a movement of a popular, self-focused culture that has generated its own metaphors and developed apart from the central tenets of traditional Christian teachings. The focus is on prosperity, upward mobility, and positive affirmations of the individual self. Sayings such as, "Man is a little god in God's class," or, "You get what you confess," represent the prosperity gospel. "Man is a little god" is a metaphor that has consequences for how we think about ourselves, about others, and about engaging the world. Remember Turner's point: the metaphors we choose to live by can make a crucial difference in our self-becoming, and in the worlds we help create or destroy. Missing in the prosperity gospel agenda are metaphors for historical and collective understandings of selfhood. It does not acknowledge the consequences of our metaphors and our moral responsibilities. Historical and collective understandings are replaced by a notion of the self as somehow autonomous and self-contained. Missing is a concern for justice, a genuine interest in discerning our complicity in the injury of others, and how all of this is related to the living web of which we are a part. Indeed, we may not see our "inescapable network of mutuality...our single garment of destiny" when our metaphors are captive to a narrow interest. When models and practices of pastoral care locate ideal images of well-being within the lone and autonomous individual (or in the family isolated from the dynamic interplay of history, culture, and society) rather than within interdependent and co-emerging relations, then it may not be far from supporting the tenets we associate with the prosperity gospel. Pastoral care practices that eschew context awareness and are devoid of economic, social-psychological analysis are vulnerable to reductionistic thinking. Obscured are the multivalent ecological metaphors that help us to see the various strands that constitute the relational web of which we are a part. Needed are not only extended metaphors for individual psychology, but also systemic and/or relational metaphors of how we might or ought to cooperate in weaving a better or more just and compassionate "web of life." Certain biblical metaphors may help us to think about how we might become "...repairer[s] of the breach, the restorer[s] of streets to live in"—in our time (Isa. 58:12b).

River Metaphor

The river metaphor moves us in a helpful direction. The idea of the river can help with the complexity and the processes that often mark the challenges for pastoral care in community, culture, and society. We note literally and metaphorically that there are many different kinds of rivers, with varying depths, lengths, widths, and environments. Most rivers journey to the sea. They have a common destination. They are a part of a dynamic ecological world system that recycles and renews. The sun draws the water up from the sea and forms clouds. The wind blows the clouds over the land. The clouds release the water that returns to the earth as raindrops. In the higher elevations the rain creates rivulets, which become run-off streams. Run-off streams become rivers, and, when they leave the higher elevations, they carry rocks and tree stumps that carve out riverbeds. Some of them are deep. The rivers that run in deep channels can carry boats and other cargo. The rivers twist and turn their way through the land. Sometimes they join with other rivers and become a very strong current. Then it makes its way to the sea.

A river creates a riverbank where those who play in it may rest, look upstream or downstream and reassess where they are and determine where the stream is headed. The river has a surface, but the deep undercurrents may serve as metaphor for the forces that pull us along or motivate us to move in a certain direction. We may also need to struggle against certain currents or the main flow. The rocks and tree parts are the river's tools for carving out its niche and its depth, and its heritage. Trees that are planted by a river send down deep roots. They grow big, tall, and strong.

The river, and all that it carries, encounters many different challenges as it journeys through the land toward its destination. Sometimes a river will flood, becoming destructive. The river gives life, and it can take life. Other times a river may dry up and die. The life of a river can be unpredictable, as are our own lives.

The metaphor of the river and the basic element of water is common in traditional hymns ("When Peace Like a River"), in spirituals ("Deep River") and in sacred texts (Gen. 2:10—the ancient river that flowed out of Eden; Ps. 46:4—river as streams of gladness; Mk. 1:5—the Jordan river where Jesus was baptized; John 7:38—rivers of living water; Rev. 22:1—the river of life). River metaphors are multivalent and have been used as resources for pastoral care. They work effectively as metaphor when they address unconscious behaviors, illuminate meaning in our present life situation, and help people to see new possibilities for justice and human becoming.

Metaphor only works with some conscious effort on our part. One has to be open to the possibility and power of metaphoric communication. Recently a talk show host was featuring a conversation about cancer. During the conversation one of the guests stated that it is hard to know what to say to a friend who has been diagnosed or is living with cancer. The guest was looking in vain for the right words and the right time to speak them and to never offend. He mentioned that his friend who was diagnosed with cancer asked him to pray for her. He said to the talk show host, "I am not a spiritual person, I do not pray, and so I did not know what to do with that request." The talk show host spoke up, "You do not have to pray to God; you could pray to anybody or to anything, or to yourself. Sometimes a prayer means a strong thought, or wish, or you could say, 'I will keep you in my thoughts.'" But is this really what the friend who requested help in the form of a prayer meant? Was she speaking metaphorically or literally? Had she planted a seed that might lead to a connection with the Divine? We do not know.

Precaria is the Latin root for "prayer." It means to obtain by entreaty. It is normally thought of as an address (as a petition) to God, or *a* god, in word or thought. We can also define prayer as an earnest request or wish. But to whom is such an earnest request directed? We normally direct our most earnest speech to someone in particular, someone we deem worthy of our trust. *The Oxford Compact English Dictionary* defines prayer as a request for help or expression of thanks addressed to God or another deity; an earnest hope or wish; a wish or hope for a particular outcome.[19]

Who might be the helper in a situation of existential despair, loneliness, anxiety, or cancer? Who or what can address our deepest fears in a life-threatening situation? Can it be just anybody or anything? This book answers, "No!" There is a longing for the eternal that nothing finite can satisfy. This longing for the infinite gives rise to the metaphors and to metaphoric communication. The psalmist states this longing in terms of thirst: "My soul thirsts for God, / for the living God" (Ps. 42:2).

What does prayer mean in the talk show situation above? What does one pray for? The psalmists, Turner suggests, direct all earnest requests to God, because God is the everlasting one who can deliver and strengthen us and cause songs of praise to well up from within. In the illustration above, the friend diagnosed with cancer and requesting prayer may have been asking that her friend talk to God on her behalf. The talk show guest may have thought this when he said, "I am not a spiritual person, and I do not pray." He rightly assumed that prayer implied a spiritual connection with a divine reality. But the talk show host downplayed this understanding of "prayer" to mean almost anything. "Almost anything" may not go far enough. "Almost anything" may not point us to questions of solid trust in God and the deeper quest for deliverance and redemption with which persons of faith struggle. "Almost anything" neglected the idea of the receiver of our prayers. Turner points us to the one who receives prayers when she referenced Psalm 84:8–11. God, the receiver of our prayers, is our home, the resting place where we can entrust our deepest fears, concerns, and worries. God is the one who causes happiness and strength to arise within us. God is the one who lifts up our heads when we are downcast (Ps. 27:5–6). When are words or thoughts or action a prayer? When are they not? How do we decide? Metaphorical communication can help us with these questions.

How does belief in God (vs. belief in anybody or anything) make a difference when we pray? And how do we know when God is the one who answers our prayers? These are the questions that Turner wrestles with in this volume. The object of worship makes all the difference in the world. God is responsive to human needs in a way that transcends the limited responses of human agents. The *relationship* between God, the one who prays, and the community matters. Turner uses words like "redeemer," "deliverer," "helper," "protector," "my rock," and "my salvation" to describe our ever-emerging relationship to God. The psalmist refers to God as a rock and redeemer (Ps. 18:46). The meanings of these terms are derived from everyday life and given an extended meaning and an ultimate point of reference. As metaphor, then, the term "rock" indicates something that is solid, trustworthy, and something that can hide or shield us from danger. The opposite, which could be anything or anybody, is undependable, unjust, conditional, deceptive, self-serving, transitory, limited, or fickle.

"Redeemer" carries both an immediate and familiar point of reference in the world of everyday life. It means to buy something back, to restore its value. When a company or the government invests in a community by building housing and bringing business back, then it is redeeming the land or the neighborhood. In this example, the term "redeemer" has meaning in the commercial world of everyday life. It is primarily contextualized by economic interest. Turner points us to an older and broader meaning of redemption and redeemer. As metaphor for God, the broader meanings are the ultimate reference point because they purport to speak about the human-Divine relationship in which God continues to invest. These terms also bear a relationship to one another because they purport to speak about the character of God. God the redeemer is the one who inspires and draws us out, setting our feet on rock solid ground. The God who sees, hears, and delivers is a God who cares, and sometimes weeps. This omnipresent, liberating and caring God is the fundamental reality or presence and ground for transformation in human activity. In order to talk about this God, this supreme transforming and caring presence at work in the ebb and flow of everyday life, we must use metaphoric communications.

Conclusion

We return to where we began. The skyline has changed! A big tree has fallen! This could be a metaphor for what has happened to some of our metaphors in this volume as we journey through it. When our root metaphors change, so do we. Turn, for example, to the metaphor of the comforter, in Psalm 86:17. "Comforter" implies that something went wrong and needs to be set right. It implies that our experiences are not static, but powerful, multivalent, and changing. In order to experience comfort, something must change: a correction must be brought about. Then hope will arise and healing begin. "Comfort" may also be translated as "repent." This metaphor is a direct challenge to the idea that God never changes. (Compare to Heb. 13.8.) Are repentance and change a part of the divine experience? The different and seemingly conflicting metaphors in this volume tell us that people at different times, in different places and cultures, experience things differently. Things change. Sometimes they fall apart. This expansive variety of metaphors also tells us that God is free to be God.

Some metaphors for God change or fall out of use, while others appear to endure. Others are revived. The task of the preacher is to take the differing and confusing, contradictory and commonplace events of everyday life and lift them up in such a way that we may see new possibilities in the vital Divine-human encounters. This will sometimes challenge cherished, but outworn, metaphors for God. John Hicks provides an example referring to the consequences of a certain interpretation of the Incarnation: "For Christianity's implicit or explicit claim to a unique superiority as the central focus of God's saving activity on earth, has come to seem increasingly implausible within the new global consciousness of our time."[20] Old metaphors may need to be dropped or recovered. New metaphors may arise to illuminate the vital Divine-human encounter. The idea of the fallen big tree used at the beginning of this essay may help illuminate something about God's gift to us in the life of a homiletics' professor. The ideas of a big tree fallen and the changing skyline suggest a connection with God, nature, and our own on-going work. The idea of a big tree suggests that the tree's roots are deep in the soil. It has stood tall, weathered many storms, and endured for a great while. Such a tree may remind us of wisdom and faithfulness—standing one's ground against many odds. When big trees grow tall they are vulnerable because they stand out, but they also know how to stand their ground, sturdy and strong, during a season of strong winds. They don't bend under pressure, and seem to laugh in the face of precarious conditions, unintimidated. They hold their ground for a season. Then, in time, they fall and make room for something else. This is a part of the human condition. The skyline changes, but something universal, enduring, and timeless remains, and we are a part of it.

Notes

Introduction

[1]See E. A. Hermanson, "Recognizing Hebrew Metaphors: Conceptual Metaphor Theory and Bible Translation," *Journal of Northwest Semitic Languages* vol. 2, no. 22 (1996): 67–78. Hermanson discusses the complexity in deciding what is and what is not metaphor in the Old Testament. For a similar discussion, see David H. Aaron, *Biblical Ambiguities: Metaphor, Semantics and Divine Imagery* (Leiden, Boston, Koln: Brill, 2001).

[2]See Roger Hazelton, "Theology and Metaphor," *Religion in Life* vol. 1, no. 46 (1977): 7–21. Hazelton explains that metaphors are proposals for belief that are to be contemplated as possibility. Also see Peter W. Macky, *The Centrality of Metaphors to Biblical Thought: A Method for Interpreting the Bible* (Lewiston/Queenston/Lampeter: The Dewin Mellen Press, 1990), who defines metaphor and provides a method for identifying biblical metaphors in all their varieties.

[3]Though we will not be discussing them in this volume, there is another category of metaphor used extensively in the Old Testament. These are the metaphors that ascribe to God human physical attributes and characteristics—face, ear, eye, eyelids, mouth, lips, arms, palms, fingers, feet, hands, etc. For a listing of these metaphors, see Martin Klingbeil, *Yahweh Fighting from Heaven: God as Warrior and as God of Heaven in the Hebrew Psalter and Ancient Near Eastern Iconography* (Gottingen: Vandenhoeck & Ruprecht, 1999), 30.

[4] See David Penchansky, *What Rough Beast: Images of God in the Hebrew Bible* (Louisville: WJKP, 1999), who discusses "The Insecure God, The Irrational God, The Vindictive God, The Dangerous God, The Malevolent God, and The Abusive God."

[5]Terence E. Freitheim, "Some Reflections on Brueggemann's God," in *God in the Fray: A Tribute to Walter Brueggemann,* ed. Tod Linnafelt and Timothy K. Beal (Minneapolis: Fortress, 1998), 24–29.

[6]Henri Blocher, "Divine Immutability," in *The Power and Weakness of God,* ed. Nigel M. De S. Cameron (Edinburgh: Rutherford House Books, 1989), 3–6.

[7]Tod Linnafelt and Timothy K. Beal, eds., *God in the Fray: A Tribute to Walter Brueggemann* (Minneapolis: Fortress, 1998), 7.

[8]See www.bibletexts.com/glossary/names-of-god-ot.htm for fuller explanations of the variety of names for God in the Old Testament.

[9]Celine Mangan, "Whatever Happened to the Old Testament God?" *Milltown Studies* 45 (2000): 58–65. The author discusses the debate among theologians regarding portraits of God as authoritarian and violent, merciful and compassionate.

Metaphors

[1]"Anointing in the Old Testament," by Roger Cotton. http://www.agts.edu/faculty/faculty_publications/articles/cotton_anointint.pdf.

[2]Hayim Nahman Bialik and Yehoshua Hana Ravnitzky, eds., *The Book of Legends: Legends from the Talmud and Midrash,* trans. William G. Braude (New York: Schocken Books, 1992), 76–77.

[3]Mary Donovan Turner, *Old Testament Words: Reflections for Preaching* (St. Louis: Chalice Press, 2003), 67–69.

[4]Dan Vogel, "Ambiguities of the Eagle," in *Jewish Bible Quarterly* 26 (April-June 1998): 87. Vogel points out that Exodus 19:4 ("How I bore you on eagles' wings…") is the only pronouncement in which God speaks of God in poetic, metaphoric language in the Hebrew Bible.

[5]Bialik and Ravnitzky, *The Book of Legends,* 72.

[6]Turner, *Old Testament Words,* 9–14.

[7]See Deuteronomy 32:6; Jeremiah 3:4, 19; Malachi 2:10; Isaiah 63:7—64:2.

[8]See Wonyong Jung, "The Divine Father Concept in the Old Testament," Sahmyook University Monographs Doctoral Dissertation Series 5 (Seoul, Korea: Institute for Theological Research, Sahmyook University, 1997). The author indicates that divine fatherhood expresses itself in adopting, redeeming, providing for, taking care of and protecting, exercising love and compassion for, guiding, and correcting God's people.

[9]Sallie McFague, *Metaphorical Theology: Models of God in Religious Language* (Philadelphia: Fortress Press, 1982), 9.

[10]See www.gospeltrail.com/Study/God/elshaddai.htm

[11]Isaac Watts, "O God, Our Help in Ages Past," 1719.

[12]Phyllis Trible, *God and the Rhetoric of Sexuality* (Philadelphia: Fortress Press, 1978), 90.

[13]Michael Ledner, "You Are My Hiding Place," 1981.

[14]Reginald Heber, "Holy, Holy, Holy! Lord God Almighty!" 1826.

[15]Ibid.

[16]See the following sources:

- R. Amba, *Bonds of Love: Methodic Studies of Prophetic Texts with Marriage Imagery (Isa 50:1–3 and 54:1–10, Hosea 1—3, Jeremiah 2—3)* (Assen: Van Corcum, 1999). The author believes that the use of the husband/wife relationship as a metaphor for God's relationship to Israel demonstrates that God is near, makes a lasting commitment, and calls the people to respond.
- F. Rachel Magdalene, "Ancient Near Eastern Treaty Curse and the Ultimate Texts of Terror: A Study of the Language of Divine Sexual Abuse in the Prophetic Corpus," in *A Feminist Companion to the Latter Prophets* (1995), 326–50. She argues that, in the prophets, God actively participates in sexual violence against women. We must stand against these texts.
- Renita Weems, *Love: Marriage, Sex and Violence in the Hebrew Prophets*, OBT (Minneapolis: Fortress, 1995). The author indicates that the metaphor of God as an abusive husband has gone awry and has been used to justify violence against women.
- Athalya Brenner, "Pornoprophetics Revisited: Some Additional Reflections," *Journal for the Study of the Old Testament* 70 (1996): 63–86.

[17]Kathleen O'Connor, "The Tears of God and Divine Character in Jeremiah 2—9," in *God in the Fray*, 173–75.

[18]Jean Marie Hiesberger, *The Catholic Bible, Personal Study Edition:* New American Bible, 2007, 169.

The priestly blessing was also discovered on a silver amulet in a concealed burial chamber in Jerusalem. This artifact provides the earliest biblical Hebrew text ever discovered. www.denverseminary.edu/seedsofchange.

[19]See K. P. Darr, "Two Unifying Images in the Book of Isaiah," in *Uncovering Ancient Stories*, 17–30. In Isaiah the procreative ability of women is used in divine metaphor.

[20]Adelaide A. Pollard, "Have Thine Own Way, Lord!" 1902.

[21]See Turner, *Old Testament Words,* 36–39.

[22]Jerome F. D. Creach, "Yahweh as Refuge and the Editing of the Hebrew Psalter," in *JSOT Sup* 217 (Sheffield: Sheffield Academic Press, 1996).

[23]Samuel Terricn, "The Metaphor of the Rock in Biblical Theology," in *God in the Fray*, 158.

[24]See Turner, *Old Testament Words,* 66–68.

[25]See Mary Lin Hudson and Mary Donovan Turner, *Saved from Silence: Finding Women's Voice in Preaching* (St. Louis: Chalice Press, 1999), 92–93.

[26]"Go Down, Moses," African American spiritual.

[27]"We Shall Overcome," African American spiritual.

[28]In "The Tears of God and Divine Character in Jeremiah 2—9," in *God in the Fray,* 179, Kathleen O'Connor discusses the sharp discontinuity with the God who executes war and the God who weeps. See Jeremiah 8:18—9:22.

[29]Ibid., 183–85.

[30]See J. P. J. Olivier, "Rendering ydyd as a Benevolent Patron in Isaiah 5:1," *Journal of Northwest Semitic Languages* vol. 2, no. 22 (1996): 59–65. The development of a more integrated economy as well as the imposition of a taxation system in Isaiah's time demanded forms of social control among which patronage would have been effective. God is the patron who cares for and protects his clients, but who expects loyalty and allegiance from them. See also Hannes Olivier, "God as Friendly Patron: Reflections on Isaiah 5:1—7," in *Feet on Level Ground* (1996).

[31]See Hudson and Turner, *Saved From Silence,* 28.

[32]See Marc Brettler, "Images of YHWH as Warrior in the Psalms," *Semeia* 61 (1993): 136–38, who discusses Psalms 3, 46, 83, and 144 to identify the cluster of images that signify an understanding of God as warrior. According to Brittler, the warrior image (or attributes related to it) appears in three-fourths of the Psalms. Also see *Women, War and Metaphor: Language and Society in the Study of the Hebrew Bible,* ed. Claudia Camp, *Semeia* 61, (1993). This volume offers interesting articles on rape as the biblical metaphor for war, women warriors of the Old Testament, and the images of Yahweh as warrior.

[33]Or, is it time to name and reclaim violent models of God? See B. Jill Carroll, *The Savage Side: Reclaiming Violent Models of God* (Lanham, Boulder, New York, Oxford: Rowman &Littlefield Publishers, Inc., 2001).

[34]For this understanding of Jacob and the wrestler I am indebted to Athanasios Hatzopoulos, "The Struggle for a Blessing: Reflections on Genesis 32:24–31," *The Ecumenical Review* (Oct. 1996): 507–12.

Questions for Reflection

[1]John Greenleaf Whittier, "Dear Lord, and Father of Mankind," 1872.

[2]Alice Walker, *In Search of Our Mother's Gardens* (San Diego, New York, London: Harcourt Brace Jovanovich, 1970), 16.

[3]W.D. Longstaff, "Take Time to be Holy," 1882.

[4]Adelaine A. Pollard, "Have Thine Own Way, Lord," 1902.

[5]Irenaeus,*Against the Heresies IV,* Pr 4; 39,2

[6]Fanny J. Crosby, "Praise Him! Praise Him!" 1869. See also Jessie Brown Pounds, "I Know That My Redeemer Liveth," 1893.

[7]Isaac Watts, "O God, Our Help in Ages Past," 1719.

[8]Augustus M. Toplady, "Rock of Ages, Cleft for Me," 1776.

Metaphors and Ministry

[1]C. M. Turbayne extends Aristotle's definition of metaphor found in *Poetics*. See C. M. Turbayne, *The Myth of Metaphor* (South Carolina: University of South Carolina Press, 1970); Aristotle, *Poetics,* trans I. Bywater, in *The Complete Works of Aristotle: The Revised Oxford Translation,* 2 vols., section 3, part XXI, ed. Jonathan Barnes (Princeton University Press, 1984). See also Philip Barker, *Using Metaphors in Psychotherapy* (New York: Brunner/Maqzel Publishers, 1985), 5.

[2]Ian G. Barbour, *Myths, Models and Paradigms: A Comparative Study in Science and Religion* (New York: Harper and Row, Publishers, 1974), 12.

[3]George Lakoff, *Women, Fire, and Dangerous Things: What Categories Reveal about the Mind* (Chicago: The University of Chicago Press, 1987), 225.

[4]George Lakoff and Mark Johnson, *Metaphors We Live By* (Chicago: The University of Chicago Press, 1980), 3.

[5]Ibid., 5.

[6]Ibid.

⁷Sallie McFague, *Metaphorical Theology: Models of God in Religious Language* (Philadelphia: Fortress Press, 1982); id., *Speaking in Parables: A Study in Metaphor and Theology* (Philadelphia: Fortress Press, 1975).

⁸McFague, *Metaphorical Theology,* 10–14.

⁹John Hicks, *The Metaphor of God Incarnate: Christology in a Pluralistic Age* (Louisville: Westminster/John Knox Press, 1993), 1.

¹⁰Ibid., 6.

¹¹Ibid., 10.

¹²Ibid.

¹³Barker, *Using Metaphors in Psychotherapy,* 29.

¹⁴Ibid., 6.

¹⁵For an elaboration of the relational web metaphor, see Archie Smith Jr., *The Relational Self: Ethics & Therapy from a Black Church Perspective* (Abingdon Press, 1982), 53. This volume argues for a metaphor for pastoral care that recognizes a relational, social, or communal understanding of the self as a constituent member of the web of life, and for the social-intentional character of the agent as determinant in structuring justice within the life of the community and society.

¹⁶For an elaboration of the river metaphor for pastoral care, see Archie Smith Jr., *Navigating the Deep River: Spirituality in African American Families* (Cleveland: United Church Press, 1997). The river is used as a metaphor on several different levels, including the workings of the mainstream of society of which we are a part, a description of the processes of family life in the main stream that can help bind us together or tear us apart, the droplets of experience that help to constitute the experiential stream of individual life, and spirituality as a resource to be tapped and—when it is strong—can carry us through difficult times.

¹⁷"Chief Seattle's Thoughts," http://www.brainyquote.com/quotes/authors/c/chief_seattle.html. There is controversy over whether or not Chief Seattle actually spoke or wrote these words, or if they came from the hand of Ted Perry, some thirty years later and were then attributed to Chief Seattle.

¹⁸Martin Luther King Jr., *A Testament of Hope: The Essential Writings of Martin Luther King, Jr.,* ed. James Melvin Washington (San Francisco: Harper & Row, 1986), 290.

¹⁹*The Oxford Compact English Dictionary,* ed. Catherine Soanes, second edition, revised (Oxford: Oxford University Press, 2003), 889.

²⁰Hicks, *The Metaphor of God Incarnate,* 7.

Index of Biblical Citations

Genesis

2:4	62
6:6	16
15:1	12
17	29
17:1–2	41
27:28	27
28:3	41
32:24–30	86, 87
35:11	41
43:30	18
45:14	18
48:3	42
49:22–25	41

Exodus

3	36
3:7–8	36, 79
3:14	3
13:21	14
14:1–2, 30	71
15:2	71, 76
16:9	14
19:4–5	27, 29
22:21–24	65
33:11	39
33:19	70
40	9

Numbers

6:24–26	54
11	59
15:11–12	59

Deuteronomy

4:24	36, 37
5:22–25	37
10:17–18	65
14:29	65
16:11, 14	65
17:19	65

24:19–21	65
26:12, 13	65
32	32
32:4–6	32, 69
32:18	58
33:28	27

Ruth

1–4	66
1	64

I Samuel

10:1	9
15:11	16
16:1	10
16:11,12,13	10

II Samuel

22:1–4	38

I Kings

3:16–28	18
17:8–16	65
18:20–40	84

Job

37:23–24	40

Psalms

3:3	11
3:5	81
3:7	30
6:1–2	43
6:9-109	30
8:3	21
9:7–8	51
9:9	78
10:9	48
10:14	34, 35
13:1–2	30
14:6	67
16:1	68

16:2–11	60
16:5	59
17:8	72
18	23
18:1–3	2
18:3	38–39
18:16–19	24
18:19	71
18:31	68
19:4	69
21	86
22:3–5	23
22:6–8	57
22:9–10	56
22:11	57
22:19	44, 57
23	16
23:1	73
23:4	80
26:1	52
27:1	55, 82
27:5–6	82
27:13	82
29:1 -2; 3–4	84
31	46
31:1–2	68
31:4	48
31:16	54
32:5–7	45–46
33:20	11, 44
35:2	12
35:7	48
35:24	52
36:9	55
37:6	55
38:5	45
38:21	45
39:11	55
40:11	18
41:4	43

43:1	52
43:3,5	55
51:10–12	82
56:13	55
57:6	48
61:2–3	67
68:5–6	35
68:4–6	64
69:16–18	66
71	39
71:1–2, 6	24
71:22	46
77:19	17
78:40–41	79
80:3–7	54
82:3–4, 8	52
82:4–5	24
84:1–11	80,81
84:8–11	80
86:15–17	15
89:20–26	31–32
91	39, 68
91:1–4	72
91:15	80
98:9	52
103	33
103:13	19
104:18	68
115:9, 10, 11	12
116:5–8	18
118:10–14	77
119:114	46
119:135	54
121:1–2	44
139	21
140:5	48
143:3	29
144	39
147:1–3	42

Proverbs

2:6–7	11
16:7	29
23:11	67
24:17	29

Ecclesiastes

11:7	54

Isaiah

1:2	61
1:2–3	79
1:16–17	34
5:1	83
6:3, 5	47
9:17	65
12:1–2	70
12:6	47
18:4	13
25	15
25:4–5	72, 73
25:6–10	73
30:15	47
40:1	15
40:11	73
40:25	47
40:25–31	21
40:28–31	20
40:31	29
41:13, 14	45
42:14	58
45:9–10	62
46:3–4	57,58
49:13	17
49:14–15	58
49:15	19, 59
51:3	17
52:9	17
54:4–8	49
55:10–11	76
57:15	47
58:6–7	43
61:1– 2,3	9, 11
63:7	32
63:16	33
64:1	33
64:8–9	33
66:13–17	58,59

Jeremiah

3:14,22	61
4:28	16
7:5–7	34
7:6	65
8:11	44
8:18–9:1	44,80
18	62

23:4	74
31:18ff	61
42:9–10	16
49:16	70

Lamentations

1,2	31
3:58	67

Ezekiel

34:11–16	75

Hosea

2:6, 9, 14	19, 51
5:12, 15	56
6:1–3	75
6:3	22, 23
6:4	15, 26
7:11–12	48,49
11:1	60
11	20
11:8–9	61
13:3	26, 53
13:7	52, 53
13:7–8	53
14:4–6	25, 26

Amos

5:24	34–35

Obadiah

1:3	70

Micah

6:1–3	63
6:6–7	64
6:8	34, 64
7:8	54

Habakkuk

3:16	85

Zechariah

7:10	65

Malachi

3:5	65